SEMINAR STUDIES IN HISTORY

D0009794

China since 1949

LINDA BENSON

Longman

An imprint of **Pearson Education**

London · New York · Toronto · Sydney · Tokyo · Singapore · Hong Kong · Cape Town
New Delhi · Madrid · Paris · Amsterdam · Munich · Milan · Stockholm

Pearson Education Limited
Edinburgh Gate
Harlow
Essex CM20 2JE,
England

and Associated Companies throughout the world

Visit us on the World Wide Web at:
www.pearsoned.co.uk

First published in Great Britain in 2002

© Pearson Education Limited 2002

The right of Linda Benson to be identified as author
of this work has been asserted by her in accordance
with the Copyright, Designs and Patents Act 1988.

ISBN 978-0-582-35722-8

British Library Cataloguing in Publication Data
A CIP catalogue record for this book can be obtained from the British Library

Library of Congress Cataloging in Publication Data
A CIP catalog record for this book can be obtained from the Library of Congress

15 14 13 12 11
12 11 10 09

Typeset by 7 in 10/12 Sabon Roman
Printed and bound in Malaysia, PJB

The Publishers' policy is to use paper manufactured from sustainable forests.

CONTENTS

INTRODUCTION TO THE SERIES

Such is the pace of historical enquiry in the modern world that there is an ever-widening gap between the specialist article or monograph, incorporating the results of current research, and general surveys, which inevitably become out of date. *Seminar Studies in History* is designed to bridge this gap. The series was founded by Patrick Richardson in 1966 and his aim was to cover major themes in British, European and World history. Between 1980 and 1996 Roger Lockyer continued his work, before handing the editorship over to Clive Emsley and Gordon Martel. Clive Emsley is Professor of History at the Open University, while Gordon Martel is Professor of International History at the University of Northern British Columbia, Canada, and Senior Research Fellow at De Montfort University.

All the books are written by experts in their field who are not only familiar with the latest research but have often contributed to it. They are frequently revised, in order to take account of new information and interpretations. They provide a selection of documents to illustrate major themes and provoke discussion, and also a guide to further reading. The aim of *Seminar Studies in History* is to clarify complex issues without over-simplifying them, and to stimulate readers into deepening their knowledge and understanding of major themes and topics.

A NOTE ON ROMANIZATION AND PRONUNCIATION OF CHINESE WORDS

Chinese terms, names, and places in this book are romanized according to the *pinyin* system which has generally replaced the earlier form (Wade-Giles). Therefore, the older spellings of *Peking, Chiang Kai-shek* and *Mao Tse-tung* appear in these pages as Beijing, Jiang Jieshi and Mao Zedong.

For English speakers, the new form has the advantage of being easier to read and pronounce since the sound of most consonants and vowels is close to the corresponding English letter, with some exceptions, listed below.

c = a combination of z and s
q = ch
x = sh
zh = j as in Joe

ACKNOWLEDGEMENTS

It is a pleasure to acknowledge and thank the many colleagues and friends who have helped me over the years to understand the dramatic changes that have taken place in China since 1949. Although too numerous to mention individually their collective wisdom and scholarly endeavors remain a source of inspiration. Special thanks are due to the series editor, Gordon Martel, whose patience as I revised my 'final' drafts was much appreciated, and to Colin Mackerras who suggested that I write the book in the first place. To all of those at Pearson Education who worked on the final editing and production of the book, I also extend my sincere thanks.

Many of my students in introductory and advanced courses on China played a role greater than they may ever know in helping to frame some of the discussion in the text. Former students who have gone on to work, travel and study in China have also contributed by letting me share, via e-mail, in their personal discovery of an Asia much changed from my own first experiences there. Special thanks to Jacqueline O'Connor who is 'our girl on Taiwan,' and to Erika, Jeni, Jackie, Matthew and Christy.

I also gratefully acknowledge the loving support of my family; my parents, Ben and Margaret Benson; my sister Nancy; my brother Douglas, and sister-in-law Dorothy Wu Ching-song. I take special pride in my nieces, Julia and Jessica, and my nephew, Eric, all of whom share Asian roots.

My husband, David Maines, provides me with daily doses of support and inspiration. He has also brought into my life his own wonderful family, including our grandchildren, Ellen and David. We not only take pride in them and our nieces and nephews, abut also – whether we deserve to or not – in all the young people and their parents who have populated our lives and, from time to time, our house: Lizzie, Hanah, Matthew, Luke, Jess, Kamran, Qian, Karima, Omar, and Abbas. This new generation of scholars, adventurers and entrepreneurs will, hopefully, share a world in which young people in China and the United States are free to shape their own new routes to international friendship and understanding.

PUBLISHERS' ACKNOWLEDGEMENTS

The publishers are grateful to the following for permission to reproduce copyright material:

Maps 1 and 2 reprinted with permission from *Current History* magazine, September 1997, © 1997 Current History, Inc.; Document 18 from *Newsweek*, 29 June 1998, © 1998 Newsweek, Inc. All rights reserved. Reprinted by permission.

McGraw-Hill for an extract from *The China Reader: People's China* by David Milton, Nancy Milton and Franz Schurmann; Random House, Inc for an extract from *Bringing Down the Great Wall* by Fang Lizhi translated by J. Williams published by Alfred A. Knopf ©1991 by Fang Lizhi; Review Publishing Company Limited for extracts from "Diplomacy of the dollar" by Bruce Gilley and Murray Hiebert published in *Far Eastern Economic Review* 10th May 2001, and "Selling the burden" by Susan V. Lawrence published in *Far Eastern Economic Review* 18th February 1999; Simon and Schuster Adult Publishing Group for an extract from *Chinese Civilization: A Sourcebook* second edition by Patricia Buckley Ebrey published by The Free Press © 1993 Patricia Buckley Ebrey; University of California Press for extracts from *Fanshen: A Documentary of Revolution in a Chinese Village* by William Hinton, and *To the Storm: The Odyssey of a Revolutionary Chinese Woman* by Daiyun Yue and Carolyn Wakeman © 1985 The Regents of the University of California; and University of Chicago Press for an extract from *Women, the Family and Peasant Revolution in China* by Kay Ann Johnson translated from a Chinese government pamphlet of 1950 on the 17-point agreement between Tibet and China.

In some cases we have been unable to trace the owners of copyright material and we would appreciate any information that would enable us to do so.

CHRONOLOGY

1949

10 January	Final battle between the CCP and the Nationalists ends in victory for the CCP
September	CPPCC convenes in Beijing to pass the Common Program
1 October	Mao declares the establishment of the People's Republic of China; 1 October becomes China's National Day

1950

February	Mao and Stalin sign the Treaty of Alliance and Friendship
April	New marriage law is announced
June	North Korea invades South Korea
	Land reform begins in rural China
October	UN troops drive into North Korea toward the Chinese border
	Chinese troops enter Tibet
November	North Korean and Chinese troops force UN troops back into southern Korea

1951

April	Douglas MacArthur is recalled from Korea; cease-fire discussions result in an agreement but fighting continues
	The 17-Point Agreement between Tibet and China is signed

1953

January	China's First Five Year Plan begins
February	Plans to begin the first mutual aid teams are announced
July	Truce is signed between North and South Korea

1954

September	China's first constitution is promulgated

1955

November	Membership in Agricultural Producers Cooperatives reaches 41% of peasant-farmers

1956

September   Eighth National People's Congress meets for the first time in eleven
               years; total CCP membership reaches 10.7 million

December   Membership of peasant-farmers in Agricultural Producers
               Cooperatives reaches 96%

1957

April–May   The '100 Flowers Campaign', to encourage discussion of policies and
               implementation since 1949, begins

June–August   The Anti-Rightist Campaign is launched against those critical of the
               CCP in the 100 Flowers Campaign

1958

May   The Great Leap Forward is formally adopted; communes form in
               rural areas of China

1959

March   Tibetan revolt; Dalai Lama flees Tibet; both sides abrogate the
               17-Point Agreement

April   Liu Shaoqi replaces Mao as China's head of state

June   Khrushchev withdraws Soviet support and criticizes Mao's plans for
               the Great Leap Forward, deepening the split between the two
               Communist states and leading to the withdrawal of Soviet advisers

July   CCP leadership meets at Lushan to discuss the Great Leap policies;
               Mao's criticism of Peng Dehuai leads to the latter being ousted from
               all positions of power

               The 'three bitter years' begin as shortages in rural and urban China
               become apparent

1962

May   Extreme deprivation leads over 100,000 Kazaks and Uighurs to flee
               Xinjiang for the USSR

August   Mao calls for 'rectification' to rebuild the CCP and launches what
               becomes known as the Socialist Education Campaign

1966

February   Mao's wife, Jiang Qing, becomes cultural adviser to the military and
               forms a political alliance with Lin Biao

July   Mao swims in the Yangzi River in his first public appearance in
               many months

August	Mao calls for a 'cultural revolution' and launches the Great Proletarian Cultural Revolution
	Thousands of young Red Guards visit Beijing to glimpse Mao
October	Attacks in the Chinese press against unnamed 'capitalist roaders'
	Wall posters denounce cadres accused of being against the revolution; violence in China escalates

1967

August	Beginning in August and lasting through to July 1968, revolutionary committees are formed to replace regular governments at all levels
	Violence continues

1969

April	The CCP Central Committee declares the Cultural Revolution to be a great success; Liu Shaoqi is officially dismissed from all posts and expelled from the CCP; Lin Biao is declared Mao's successor
June–August	Fighting erupts between Soviet and Chinese troops on China's northwestern and northeastern borders

1971

July	Henry Kissinger visits Beijing to arrange President Nixon's visit to China
October	The UN votes to recognize the People's Republic of China as the only government of China; the UN seat held by the Taiwan-based Republic of China and a place on the Security Council are both transferred to the PRC
12–13 September	The '571 Affair' in which Lin Biao, Minister of Defense, is reportedly to have led a coup attempt against Mao, shocks the Chinese public

1972

February	American President Richard Nixon visits China and signs the Shanghai Communiqué

1975

July	Jiang Jieshi dies; his son, Jiang Jingguo assumes the presidency of the Republic of China, Taiwan

1976

8 January	Death of Zhou Enlai
July	Death of Zhu De
26 July	Tangshan earthquake, south of Beijing, kills over 240,000 people

9 September	Death of Mao Zedong
6 October	Hua Guofeng announces the arrest of Mao's widow and her three closest supporters, collectively known as the 'Gang of Four'

1978

	The new constitution is announced
December	Posters critical of Deng Xiaoping appear on Democracy Wall in central Beijing

1979

1 January	The United States recognizes the Beijing government as the official government of China and withdraws recognition from Taiwan
28 January	Deng Xiaoping visits the United States
29 March	Wei Jingsheng is arrested
October	Wei is sentenced to 15 years' imprisonment

1980

7 September	Hua Guofeng is removed from office; Zhao Ziyang becomes Premier
September	New marriage law requires the use of contraception; the limiting of family size to one child officially begins
November	Trial begins of the Gang of Four

1981

25 January	Formal verdict condemns the Gang of Four
April	Hu Yaobang succeds Hua Guofeng as CCP Chairman

1984

July	Britain and China reach a settlement on the return of Hong Kong to China; final document is signed on 19 December 1984

1985

September	The start of student demonstrations calling for government reforms on university campuses in major Chinese cities; demonstrations erupt periodically until June 1989

1988

February	Jiang Jingguo, President of Taiwan, dies, and is succeeded by his Vice President, Li Denghui
25 March	Li Peng is named Premier of China by the National People's Congress Organic Law of Villagers Committees put into effect

1989

15 April	Hu Yaobang dies; students honor him by gathering in Tiananmen Square, thus beginning 'Beijing Spring'
22 April	Demonstrations expand; some 100,000 people gather in Tiananmen Square
26 April	Students in Beijing are denounced as conspirators in an editorial in the *People's Daily*
15 May	Mikhail Gorbachev arrives in Beijing
18 May	Students meet in televised exchange with CCP leaders
20 May	Martial law is imposed in Beijing
24 May	Zhao Ziyang is dismissed as Secretary-General of the CCP; he is officially removed from all official positions the following month
4 June	Tiananmen Square massacre as PLA troops clear demonstrators from the center of Beijing
23 June	Jiang Zemin, mayor of Shanghai, is officially named Secretary-General of the CCP, replacing Zhao Ziyang

1991

Collapse of the USSR; independence of Central Asian republics is declared

1994

December	Construction begins on the Three Gorges Dam project, on the western reaches of the Yangzi River; estimated cost US$30 billion and estimated construction time of 14 years to build the world's largest hydroelectric dam

1997

19 February	Deng Xiaoping dies
1 July	Hong Kong is returned to Chinese control
October	Jiang Zemin visits the United States

1998

Zhu Rongji becomes Premier, with responsibility to deepen the economic reforms begun by Deng Xiaoping

State Environment Protection Administration is established

1999

April	10,000 members of the spiritual movement, *Falungong*, or Wheel of the Law, hold a silent demonstration in Beijing

10 May	Protestors, angry over the accidental bombing of the Chinese embassy in Belgrade, stone the American embassy in Beijing
22 July	*Falungong* movement is banned
December	Macao, Portuguese controlled since 1557, is returned to China

2000

February	America grants China permanent normal trade relations, paving the way for China to enter the WTO
March	China issues warnings over the possible victory of the DPP in the Taiwan elections
	Chen Shuibian, of the DPP, wins election to the presidency of Taiwan, marking the first time the Nationalist Party loses control of that office since 1949
June	Kim Dae Jung of South Korea meets with Kim Jong Il of North Korea in the first ever such meeting between North and South

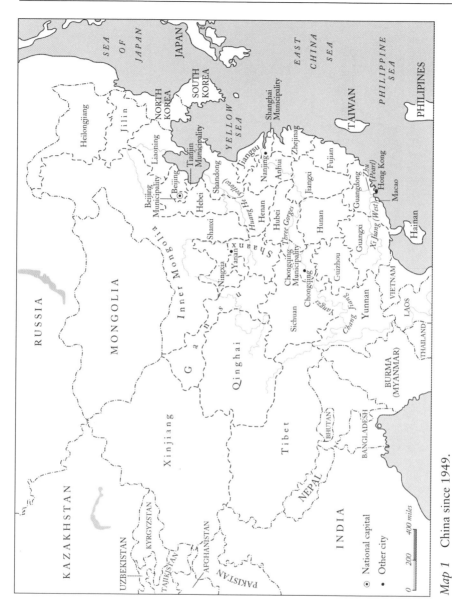

Map 1   China since 1949.
Reprinted with permission from *Current History* magazine, September 1997. © 1997, Current History, Inc.

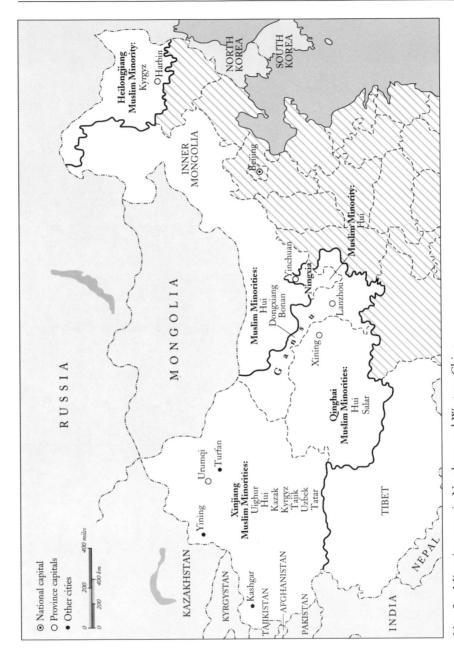

Map 2   Minority areas in Northern and Western China.
Reprinted with permission from *Current History* magazine, September 1997. © 1997, Current History, Inc.

PART ONE CHINA'S PAST

CHAPTER ONE

GENERAL INTRODUCTION

One of the most remarkable stories of the last century is the emergence of China as a modern economic giant, poised at the beginning of the twenty-first century to become a great world power. During the first half of the twentieth century, millions of rural and urban Chinese lived in poverty, struggling to survive in a country which was continually torn by war and domestic upheaval. But since that time, China has undergone a dramatic transformation. It has embraced the technological advances of the late twentieth century and has provided new opportunities for millions of Chinese to improve their lives. While problems have accompanied this transformation, China's future holds unprecedented prosperity for 1.3 billion Chinese and the promise of enhanced international status for the government that is making this possible.

The route to China's success has been as tortuously uneven as it has been rapid. China's history since 1900 – the first fifty years of which are summarized in Part Two, below – has been punctuated by natural and man-made disasters, arrogant leadership, disastrous policy decisions, and incomprehensible disregard for the welfare of millions. The early years under Communist leadership brought important changes, but only since 1978 has the ruling Communist Party found more workable solutions to the challenges which have plagued the government and people for the past 200 years.

This account of modern China since 1949 seeks to provide the student and general reader with a brief survey of the major events that mark the transition of China to a rapidly modernizing power in the space of five decades. Although the story of the Chinese Communist Party (hereafter CCP) is a central part of modern China's history, and thus is one component of the present work, this book also records the impact of CCP policies on ordinary people's lives. It shows how the majority of the population managed to accommodate some of the more extreme phases of the CCP's radical political agenda through 1976 and then turns to the impact of recent reforms on all groups and classes. In particular, it follows some of the most important changes for women and minorities since 1949.

Although members of both categories would agree that the changes have been significant, overall much remains to be done before either group attains equal opportunity to pursue education and employment.

Periodization for this book departs from the standard treatment in most texts on modern China. The initial attempts of the CCP to legitimize its rule in China and its early, highly ambitious policies are outlined in Chapter 3, which covers the period from 1949 to 1957. When these policies failed to bring about the kind of revolutionary society that the new leaders envisioned, the revolution entered a much more radical stage. The most extreme leftist period was between 1958 and 1969 when China was thrown into turmoil, as the ageing leadership sought to hasten the transformation of its country into a socialist paradise. Unfortunately, economic plans and political campaigns proved disastrous. Instead of moving China forward, the economy slowed, and the modest gains of the early years were threatened. Politically-generated violence in the 1960s' Cultural Revolution left its mark on the economic system as well as on thousands of Party faithful who found themselves excoriated and ousted from their positions of influence. Ordinary citizens were at the mercy of young Red Guard units who marauded through the countryside. Although these policies and campaigns ended by the early 1970s, the radical policies of the revolution did not end until the 1976 death of Mao Zedong, Chairman of the CCP and founder of the People's Republic of China (hereafter PRC). Therefore, the period from 1958 to 1976 is treated here as a whole, and allows discussion of the radical Marxist agenda to be the focus of Chapter 4.

With the death of Mao and the discrediting of Maoist attempts at continuing revolution, the next generation of Communist leaders began the rebuilding of China, enabling its rapid shift toward a modern economy open to foreign investment and to experimentation with cultural and political forms, all of which had been anathema to the old guard under Mao. This new period of change was led by the ageing Deng Xiaoping who, unlike Mao, chose to place other, younger and better educated members of the Party at the helm of China's 'Reform Era'. Chapter 5 traces this economic transformation and its impact on different sectors of the population to 1989. It includes a reassessment of the Tiananmen Massacre of 4 June, 1989. Despite the temporary setback to the reform movement in 1989, the process of economic reorganization continued in the 1990s, an assessment of which is the focus of Chapter 6. This chapter also traces the whereabouts of the top student leaders of the 1989 student movement, members of which pursued other interests abroad in the 1990s.

Significant changes in China have resulted in new challenges to the CCP's authority. Some of these major issues are addressed in Chapter 7 and include such problems as pollution, corruption and the social inequalities that are related to China's rapid transformation.

Chapter 8 expands the focus by turning to China's relations with the world beyond Chinese borders. It begins with a discussion of the issue of Taiwan in light of the successful reintegration of Hong Kong with China as a Special Administrative Region in 1997 and the return of the Portuguese colony of Macao to Chinese control in 1999. China's entry into the World Trade Organization (hereafter WTO) and normalization of trade relations with the United States are the strongest indicators of China's emergence as an economic power on the world stage. The text concludes with an overview of the changes that have created the present society and political system.

Throughout the text, the impact of the Communist leadership's policies on specific populations, such as women and national minorities, is used to examine the ramifications of policy implementation and to illustrate the fact that much of CCP policy prior to 1976 was more reaction to events as they developed rather than careful planning to address issues systematically. Poorly thought out and even more poorly executed, policy choices led to the suffering and death of millions, an unintended but nonetheless devastating consequence.

THEMES IN RECENT CHINESE HISTORY

China's history under the leadership of the Communist Party is marked by dramatic policy shifts that affected the lives of millions of people. These changes, which originated at the top, did not follow courses anticipated by the Party, nor were the results what the Party leadership intended. As history attests, revolutions rarely lead to the kind of society that the revolutionary leadership planned, and China's history since 1949 shows that China is no exception.

The last fifty years reveal continuing tensions within the new political system and within Chinese society. Among the most important of these are:

- tradition and revolution;
- urban and rural development;
- central and regional authority;
- communism and modernization.

Tradition and Revolution

The tension between traditional Chinese culture and the new revolutionary society that the government fostered after 1949 remains a part of Chinese life in the early twenty-first century. Chinese society has clearly changed in dramatic and measurable ways, yet patterns of the past remain. One example is in patriarchal attitudes which have yet to make a full retreat.

Male children remain valued above females, as evinced in the 1990–2000 demographics which indicate a lop-sided male–female ratio. Thus, while the one-child policy (see discussion in Chapter 5) has had a great impact in China by reducing family size, the preference for male children has been little changed. The status of women is another area in which patriarchal attitudes persist. Although the various constitutions adopted in China since 1954 accorded women full equality with men, as a group women lag behind men in earnings, education levels, and employment opportunities. Furthermore, traditional folk practices such as geomancy, or *feng shui,* and the belief in kitchen gods re-emerged in some rural areas after the death of Mao, attesting to the strength of such old beliefs despite years of CCP efforts to eradicate them. As China continues to change, patterns of the past will nonetheless continue to color the society which emerges.

Rural and Urban Development

From the 1800s onwards, China's wealth was concentrated in its large urban centers, particularly those located along its coast and river valleys. After 1900, as modern industrial production expanded, urban areas grew in importance, deepening the economic disparity between rural and urban China. Despite CCP efforts to equalize rural–urban income, significant differences in living standards remained during the Maoist period (1949–76), although income levels of rural and urban China under Mao were more equal than at any time in modern history. Government-imposed limits on mobility meant less pressure on the cities as the poorly educated rural population – some 70% of China's total – remained in the countryside. However, after Mao's death, the standard of living rose more quickly in the cities. As the reforms progressed in the 1990s, urban residents enjoyed a per capita income double that of rural areas. Eased restrictions on travel and, to some extent, on residency requirements led increasing numbers of poor men and women to China's cities. Many took whatever work was available and moved from town to town as necessary. This 'floating population' (see discussion in Chapter 7) is dramatic evidence of the income disparity which has emerged during the reforms and constitutes a major challenge for the CCP.

Central and Regional Authority

The great differences between rural and urban China also relate to different agendas of regional and central authorities. Initially, the CCP kept power centralized at Beijing and strengthened that central authority through many of its policies under Mao. Provincial governments conformed to central directives during the Maoist period as the Party imposed agricultural reforms and then moved quickly to the commune system. Under the reforms of the Deng government, however, more leeway was given to provincial and regional officials, particularly with regard to investment and economic development. Areas in advantageous geographical positions quickly benefited from the changes. The result was that the aggressive and wealthier provinces of the coast grew rich while those in the poorer hinterland fell further behind, causing the rural–urban income gap to widen, as noted above. As the economy de-centralized, control also decreased in some areas of policy, although the government kept a tight rein on banking and currency. Greater economic freedom may translate into more provincial and regional ability to deviate from CCP-mandated policies in the future. If so, as some observers suggest, the CCP could soon find itself facing regional power bases that might threaten the unity of the Chinese state. To forestall such a development, the Party is focusing on modernization and economic development funded from the national level to help it maintain power.

Communism and Modernization

From the beginning, the PRC's goal was to bring both communism and modernization to China. Maoist economic plans, initially borrowed from the USSR, sought to make China a strong, modern state, and that required an aggressive modernization agenda. However, as described in the next chapters of this book, Maoist modernization made only halting progress and at times appeared to move backwards, not forwards. From 1958 to 1976, revolution took precedence over modernization, as Mao enjoined China's people to be 'more Red [Communist] than expert'. A new period began under Mao's successor, Deng Xiaoping. After 1978, modernization became the single most important goal of the regenerated CCP. This shift away from the Maoist vision constitutes the most dramatic historical moment in China's history since 1949. Long delayed, China's modernization has at last moved into high gear, and these new successes are also giving new life to the CCP in an age when few communist-led states have managed to survive.

In the year 2000, as the CCP entered its second half-century, the original CCP goals of a strong nation with a modernized yet essentially socialist economy were recast to stress modernization bolstered by nationalism. The success of the reform period has placed China among the world's top economies in terms of size (but not in per capita income), and a majority of the Chinese people appear satisfied with these newest changes, despite the fact that this success has led to new problems.

Does economic freedom portend the collapse of the CCP? At the turn of the twenty-first century, the CCP clearly retained a firm hold over the administrative apparatus. The Party's new appeal to nationalism (see discussion below) and a widespread reluctance to take a chance on political reforms that might slow economic growth suggest that it will be some time before the CCP relinquishes its authority. Much will depend on the government's ability to overcome the problems which accompany its continuing reforms, as discussed in later chapters.

These tensions remain key elements in China today and provide the framework for examining, in the following chapters, the policies which have reshaped contemporary Chinese society in ways that the revolutionary old guard of the pre-1949 days certainly could not have anticipated as they struggled for uncertain victory.

TERMS AND CONCEPTS

Modern China has been marked by the growth of Chinese nationalism which, in 1900, was a nascent force in the movement toward revolution. In the 1990s, an appeal to nationalism marked CCP efforts to unite China's citizens under communist leadership, replacing the Marxist rhetoric of previous decades and indicating a maturation of Chinese nationalism. Because nationalism has had such a great impact on China, it is important to clarify its meaning as used in the text, along with other important forces, such as Marxism, socialism and communism, all of which are discussed briefly in this section.

'Nationalism' emerged in nineteenth-century Europe as an outgrowth of competitive nation-states and referred to pride in the history and culture of one's nation, a term which was in turn defined as a group of people with common language, territory, history and culture, separated from other neighboring peoples by virtue of a unique set of characteristics. The fact that most European peoples were historically a mixture of peoples, languages and cultures was no obstacle to governments intent on fostering nationalism, which was accomplished through the fora of print media and state-sponsored education. Nationalist slogans impressed upon citizens the importance of their particular heritage and their distinctiveness, and served to unite the people of each nation-state in ways not previously possible.

A corollary useful to ambitious states was that a nation was entitled to its 'traditional' lands. As most boundaries in Europe were established through war at one time or another, disputes over what land belonged to which nation were intensified by the doctrine of nationalism which, in its most extreme form, justified war to regain land and reach a nation's 'natural boundaries'.

The notion of nationalism was exported to the developing world of the twentieth century. In China, this European notion was embraced by the Father of the Revolution, Dr Sun Zhongshan (see below), who believed that a lack of nationalism held the Chinese people back; he urged the widespread adoption of nationalism through his 'Three Principles', which were to guide the country into the republican era. Several of the events described below indicate the spread of this new concept in early twentieth-century China. China's Communist Party came to power in part because of its embrace of modern Chinese nationalism, which remains an important component of the Communist movement in China today.

Socialism and communism were two additional Western imports that had enormous impact on modern China. Based on the teaching of Karl Marx (1818–88), Marxism, socialism and communism all called for an egalitarian economic and social system. Under socialism, the 'means of production', such as factories and agricultural land, would be owned and operated by the people themselves, who would share equally in the profits. Homes and personal property would remain privately owned. Under communism, a utopian ideal, no private ownership would be needed as all social and economic differences would be erased, along with authority of any kind. Although Marx viewed communism as the inevitable culmination of human social organization, he also wrote of revolution as the means by which the working class would gain the power to remold society into a communist paradise. In that ultimate state, the need for government apparatus itself would disappear, thus guaranteeing total equality and freedom for all.

Both socialism and communism emerged during the industrial revolution, which gave rise to a wealthy class of capitalists whose great fortunes derived from the low wages and mass production techniques of the age. Long working hours in terrible conditions of noise and dirt brought only subsistence to workers while generating huge profits for factory owners. The enormous gap between rich and poor led Marx to examine the historical evolution of the phenomenon and ultimately to the call for world-wide revolution to free the workers from their miserable lives. For some intellectuals and political activists, the term 'capitalist' personified the evils of the age. The activities of socialist and communist organizers deepened social divisions and radicalized the struggle between the growing urban labor force and the wealthy factory owners.

The exploitative conditions facing workers in China at the turn of the twentieth century mirrored the conditions of European workers. But because many factories in China were foreign owned – by Europeans and Japanese – early union organizing also tended to be nationalistic. Because much of the early union movement was led by members of the CCP, nationalism became an intrinsic part of Chinese communism. Although the Nationalist Party, first under Dr Sun and then under Jiang Jieshi, attempted to use nationalism to boost support for its programs, it would be the Communist Party that co-opted nationalism for its own cause, first in its union organizing and then by waging effective guerrilla warfare against

Japan during the Second World War. The founding of the PRC was presented as a victory of the Chinese nation, and successive PRC policies repeatedly called upon the people to sacrifice for the good of the country. Although nationalistic appeals remained an aspect of the Party's rhetoric, internal politics pushed nationalism to one side as the CCP focused on domestic problems. However, in the 1990s the CCP returned to a strongly nationalistic stance which was used to bolster flagging support for the Party, once more linking communism and nationalism in the service of the ruling Party. As an emerging economic power, China is also finding nationalism a useful tool as it competes for trading advantages and greater international power. As demonstrated in the following pages, the forces of revolution, nationalism, socialism and communism continue to shape an increasingly wealthy and powerful modern China.

CHAPTER TWO

GEOGRAPHICAL AND HISTORICAL BACKGROUND

GEOGRAPHY

China covers over 9.5 million square kilometers (3.7 million square miles), making it approximately the size of the continental United States. Unlike America, which has a population of 260 million, China's population in 2000 exceeded 1.3 billion, the largest population in the world under a single government. Exacerbating the impact of such a large number of people is the fact that the majority live on less than 40% of China's territory. The reason for this lies in China's extremely varied topography. Large expanses of the land are covered with deserts such as the Gobi and the Takla Makan, or high mountains, such as those of the Tibetan plateau. Historically, these areas were only part of the Chinese empire for short periods of time; their inclusion as a part of today's China is a direct result of the expansion of the last dynasty which was able to conquer and hold the regions now known as Inner Mongolia, Xinjiang, Tibet and Qinghai (see Map 1). To distinguish these newer additions from the core of traditional Chinese territory, the term 'China proper' is used to refer to provinces which have been part of China for over 2000 years.

The major river systems of China proper include the Huang He (Yellow River) in the north, the Chang Jiang (also called the Yangzi) in central China, and the Xi Jiang (West River) in the south. All three rivers flow west to east, allowing for relative easy transport from the hinterland to the coast. These river systems sustain millions of Chinese, who have cultivated fields watered by these rivers for hundreds of years. Agriculture in the north supplies wheat and other hard grains, while the area from the Chang Jiang south grows rice and tea, products long associated with Chinese civilization.

Given China's varied topography, the country has abundant natural resources. Coal, oil, natural gas and many kinds of ore are found across the country, and some of these deposits – oil in particular – are only now being systematically tapped. Cotton and silk have been produced for over 4,000 years by the Chinese and continue to be important exports. Modern manufacturing draws on this abundance of natural resources.

Another great asset is the population itself. Innovative, inventive, and creative, the Chinese have made invaluable contributions to the world's people, including the invention of paper, the compass, the water mill, printing, paper currency, and gun powder. In the arts and literature, China's people have left a remarkable record of creative achievement and, after emerging from the relative isolation imposed during the Maoist era, are again contributing to the world's cultural life through film, literature and the fine arts.

HISTORICAL OVERVIEW

China's long-recorded history stretches back over 4,000 years. Its imperial system of government emerged from a series of small kingdoms based in the area of the Huang He in north China. In 221 BCE, the ruler Qin Shi Huangdi unified the small states and gave his name to the new dynasty, the Qin, from which we derive the name China. He was the first ruler to use the title emperor which remained in use in China until 1912.

Although the Qin dynasty was brief (it ended not long after Qin Shi Huangdi's death in 210 BCE), successive dynasties built on Qin successes. The Han ruling family, which followed the Qin, retained the Qin administrative system but re-established the influence of Confucian ideals that stressed education and responsibility among government officials. The Han (206 BCE–220 CE) proved a successful and long-lived dynasty, gradually expanding the boundaries of the Chinese empire toward the south.

Over the centuries that followed, the imperial system held together remarkably well, welding the population together through a strong, centralized administration and a shared value system, based in Confucian teachings. While China was periodically torn by the upheavals that attended the rise and fall of the 25 major dynasties, or ruling houses which have governed China, the reconstituted imperial state would re-emerge, building on the institutions and practices of the past but also adding new contributions to China's varied historical record.

By the time of the last of these dynasties, the Qing (1644–1912), China controlled more territory than at any time in its past. It not only controlled China proper and the lands of Tibet and the far northwest, it also held sway over the neighboring states of Korea, Mongolia, and Viet Nam. The Manchu elite of the Qing ruled a multi-ethnic empire comprised of many peoples and cultures, and to their credit they held their far-flung empire together with skill into the nineteenth-century.

Around 1800, however, the dynasty began a slow, inexorable decline. Pressure to open its borders to traders from England and other European states led to military confrontation in the two Opium Wars of the middle of the nineteenth century. In both, China was the loser. It was forced to grant not only trading privileges and legal importation of British India-grown opium, but also to cede parts of its territory to European powers, opening the age of Western imperialism in East Asia. Furthermore, internal rebellion nearly toppled the dynasty between 1850 and 1864, and although the Qing defeated the rebels, they were unable to forestall the continuing decline of their military and political power. Reluctantly, the Qing rulers embarked on limited reforms in the early twentieth century, but these were too little too late. By 1911, reformers and revolutionaries looked for more radical and more rapid reform than the Manchus wished to offer. On 10 October 1911, an insurrection began at Wuhan, in central China, and quickly spread across China. When top Qing military commanders refused Qing orders to suppress the movement, the fate of the dynasty was sealed.

The new republican government which replaced the dynasty was led by Dr Sun Zhongshan, a southerner who had been educated in what was then British Hawaii. A medical doctor by training and a Christian as a result of his British education, Dr Sun dedicated his life to the idea of a republican government in his homeland. However, within the first months of his provisional presidency, divisions surfaced between the revolutionaries, leading to a transfer of power to General Yuan Shikai, a former Qing dynasty general who had belatedly joined the revolutionary forces in 1911. Yuan's government proved oppressive and the republic which emerged was far from the ideal of Sun and other leaders whose hopes were frustrated by Yuan's reactionary government. Yuan's death in 1916 momentarily opened the way for a more democratic system, but although the central government at Beijing continued to proclaim its authority, power quickly devolved to regional military leaders, popularly referred to as warlords. These men constituted the *de facto* government of China as they vied for the opportunity to assume control of the central government.

During the period of warlord power (1916–28), young Chinese began to search for a political system that could address the division and instability in China and tackle the seemingly unsolvable domestic problems of rural poverty and economic decline. The weak government of the new republic had entered the First World War in the hope of resolving issues related to the old treaty system which was still in force, but the Treaty of Versailles which ended the war simply affirmed European colonial possessions and privileges in China. Worse, in the view of many Chinese, was the fact that the treaty allowed Japan to assume the former privileges of defeated Germany, thereby giving Japan a stronger foothold in China. In May 1919, young intellectuals in China's urban centers rose in protest over the possibility that the government would accept these humiliating terms. On 4 May, thousands of students and professors took to the street of Beijing and other major cities in protest. This outpouring of nationalistic fervor was symbolic of China's struggle to find a political form. The eventual success of the demonstrators in forcing the central government to repudiate the treaty signaled the emergence of a political role for students which would be echoed in successive decades.

It was during this period of intellectual upheaval that the Chinese Communist Party was founded in 1921. Few among the 50 or so founding members could have envisioned that their Party would come to dominate China in less than 30 years. The new Party was the creation of China's new generation of activist students and professors, who looked to revolutionary political philosophies of the West to resolve China's seemingly unsolvable problems. Guided at first by members of the USSR's newly organized Comintern, the young CCP joined forces with the Nationalist Party, which was still under the leadership of Dr Sun, in 1923. This short-lived alliance dissolved soon after Sun's death in 1925 as the ambitious Jiang Jieshi assumed control of the military arm of the Nationalist movement.

As the Nationalist commander-in-chief, Jiang began a highly successful campaign, the Northern Expedition, to defeat the warlords in 1926, just a year after the death of Dr Sun; by 1927 he and his army effectively controlled China south of the Yangzi River and in the spring of that year took the city of Shanghai, with the aid of Communist Party allies. However, Jiang distrusted CCP intentions and in a sudden coup attempted to eliminate CCP members of the movement. Although some CCP members escaped Shanghai's 'White Terror' of 12 April 1927, hundreds ultimately died as Jiang ordered a bloody eradication campaign which continued through the summer (Mackerras, 1998: 44–5). The leaders of Sun's Nationalist Party relieved Jiang of his command, but without his leadership, the Northern Expedition foundered. In the winter of 1928, Jiang was recalled; in return for his continuing the military struggle, he was made provisional president of the Republic. By the summer of 1928, Jiang had either defeated or co-opted the remaining warlords and central China was reunified under his control. The CCP was now a banned organization, as were the union movements which had thrived under Communist leadership.

The defeat of the warlords and the reunification of much of the country did not resolve major issues facing China – a weak economy, great rural poverty, and widespread corruption and crime. Policies to address these and other issues were slow to evolve; new laws aimed at more equitable land holding and limits on land rents, for example, were not enforced, leaving millions to struggle at subsistence level. Much of Jiang's energies focused instead on the CCP which, although now underground, had made headway among impoverished peasant-farmers. Large CCP bases emerged in south and central China, and Jiang's military campaigns against these bases became his top priority. As a result, he left northeastern China, or Manchuria, open to Japanese attack, which came in 1931. To deal with this threat, Jiang signed a truce with Japan, enabling him to continue his campaigns against the Communists but costing him the Manchurian region, one of China's most industrially advanced areas.

Between 1927 and 1934, the CCP remained under the guidance of the Comintern. The official policy or 'line' at that time was to continue with efforts toward revolution among the urban proletariat. This policy was increasingly untenable, however, and gradually the top Soviet-trained leaders and their Soviet advisers moved to the safety of the rural Communist bases. Among the largest of these was the Jiangxi Soviet, in southeastern China's most remote and poverty-stricken counties. Here, a young leader named Mao Zedong had risen to prominence. In 1931, he was named President of the Soviet, although he was not then the head of the Communist Party. His government relied on the efforts of peasants, not urban workers or intellectuals, for Mao had already determined that the peasant-farmer, not the urban industrial worker, should be the basis of China's Communist revolution.

During the fifth of Jiang's 'Encirclement and Annihilation Campaigns' against the Communists, Jiang's army threatened to overrun Mao's Jiangxi base. The leaders voted to retreat, and in the fall of 1934 they began what came to be known as the 'Long March' which lasted until the end of 1935. Criss-crossing western China on a year's trek that covered over 6,000 miles, this retreat took an enormous toll: 90% of the 100,000 people who began the march died or deserted as the CCP took beating after beating. At a pivotal meeting in January 1935, held at the town of Zunyi, the CCP rejected the leadership of the Soviet-trained members of the Party who were blamed for the disaster. The Zunyi conference marked the beginning of Mao's rise to leadership of the movement, which he firmly assumed by 1936.

Although badly mauled in the Nationalist onslaught, battered units of CCP began to gather at a new base, in the poor inland province of Shaanxi, west of the Yellow River. Here they rebuilt their movement on the eve of the Second World War. Land reform and other policies rewarded local peasant supporters and the area under Communist control began to grow.

The full-scale invasion of China by Japan in 1937 forced Jiang and his government to face the Japanese who had used their base in Manchuria to expand into counties just north of the Great Wall and in Inner Mongolia. The early stages of the Japanese invasion began on 7 July 1937, near Beijing; soon a second front opened at Shanghai. Japanese military successes quickly mounted and by the end of the summer the major cities north of the Yellow River were in Japanese hands. By December 1937, the Japanese had successfully taken Shanghai and attacked Jiang's capital of Nanjing, which became the site of Japanese war atrocities. For over three weeks, the Japanese took revenge for Chinese resistance by brutalizing the civilian population of the city. An estimated 300,000 died in what came to be called the 'Rape of Nanjing'. Jiang and his government moved inland, to the Yangzi River city of Chongqing, where Jiang sought to hold on.

By the end of 1938, Japan occupied the major cities of eastern China and controlled the seaboard. Trapped far inland, without benefit of the production or finances of the wealthy industrial east, the Nationalist government resorted to oppressive taxation soon followed by forced military conscription. These twin evils were a nightmare for those under Nationalist control and garnered increasing ill-will for the Jiang government among all sectors of the population.

After 1941, with the entry of the United States into the war, American military aid finally began to reach the wartime capital. But only with the defeat of Japan by the Allies in 1945 was Jiang able to regain control of his country.

The end of the Second World War did not bring peace. Instead, the well-disciplined CCP and its military built on their war reputation and skillfully used propaganda to contrast its accomplishments with those of the Nationalists. They were inadvertently assisted by the poor performance of the Nationalist government in the months immediately following the Allied victory. The Nationalists' resumption of control in eastern China was marked by extreme instances of corruption as rapacious Nationalist officials amassed personal fortunes at the expense of Chinese who had endured Japanese rule or suffered the deprivations of refugee life for eight long years.

Animosity between the CCP and Nationalists also re-emerged despite American efforts at mediation. Instead of reconstruction, in 1946 China entered upon a short, brutal civil war (1946–49) with each party investing its future in the military struggle. With major contributions of American military and financial assistance, Jiang and his well-equipped army outnumbered the Communist's People's Liberation Army (PLA) by two to one. The Nationalists gained a series of quick victories and it appeared that Jiang would emerge the winner, as many observers predicted. But poor military leadership and low morale among Nationalist troops contributed to a series of devastating defeats in Manchuria in 1947–48. In a final battle of massed troops north of the Yangzi River, the PLA proved victorious. Jiang pulled back, finally retreating to a last redoubt on the island of Taiwan. There, some 2 million evacuated troops prepared for a final onslaught which never came. Instead, in the summer of 1949, the Chinese Communist Party sought to consolidate its control over the mainland, leaving aside the British colony of Hong Kong, the Portuguese colony of Macao, and the defeated men of the Nationalist Party on Taiwan.

As the country's new leader, Mao declared the establishment of the People's Republic of China on 1 October 1949, from a podium erected in front of Tiananmen, the Gate of Heavenly Peace. 'China has stood up', Chairman Mao declared, thus inaugurating a new era in Chinese history.

CHAPTER THREE

CHINA'S NEW REVOLUTIONARY ROAD, 1949–57

For a majority of China's 500 million people the 1949 Communist victory over the Nationalist forces of Jiang Jieshi was cause for celebration. Long years of war that had divided the country and brought misery and poverty to millions ended, and although there was uncertainty about the shape that the new government would take, there was reason for hope as China began a period of reconstruction. Peasants and workers who had supported the revolutionaries anticipated the beginning of a new era and the CCP moved quickly to institute changes that would reward the people's support.

The problems facing the new government were enormous. In addition to alleviating the great misery inflicted by years of warfare, the government needed to address widespread malnutrition and public health issues. Much of China's infrastructure was shattered by years of war: public and private buildings were destroyed or damaged, and roads, railways, and bridges were in ruins, making it difficult to reach many remote rural areas. The economy was reduced to a bartering system, as the old Nationalist currency, the *fabi*, was valueless. In the middle of the twentieth century, China had an estimated gross national product (GNP) per capita that was only one-third to one-half that of England in the late seventeenth century, and agricultural output still accounted for about half of the country's total GNP (Uhalley, 1988: 82–3). Further, thousands of surrendered Nationalist military units posed a potential challenge to CCP control, as did the thousands of former Nationalist supporters still in China, unable to flee to Hong Kong or Taiwan. The challenges posed by these problems would be daunting for any government; the new People's Republic faced them head-on and the immediate results were impressive, particularly given the enormity of the tasks undertaken.

THE CCP LEADERSHIP

Leading the efforts to address these issues and rebuild the country was Mao Zedong. At the age of 55, Mao held the titles of Chairman of the Chinese Communist Party, President of China, and chief military commander. As the

CCP was now the most powerful force in China, the title Chairman (of the Party) came to represent Mao's supreme status. Yet Mao was little known outside China. Only a handful of Westerners had ever met him or other top Party leaders; many Chinese had heard only vague stories about the revolutionary hero who now held the future of their country in his hands.

Who was he? As eminent historian of modern China Jonathan Spence writes, 'Mao's beginnings were commonplace, his education episodic, his talents unexceptional; yet he possessed a relentless energy and a ruthless self-confidence that led him to become one of the world's most powerful rulers' (Spence, 1999: xi). Born in the central Chinese province of Hunan in 1893, Mao was the eldest son of a prosperous farmer. Unlike the vast majority of his contemporaries, Mao received a college education. Upon his graduation in 1918, he moved to Beijing and met China's leading Marxists at Beijing University. When the CCP was founded in 1921, Mao was one of the youngest members. The direction of his life was fixed thereafter in the cause of Communist victory. He supported himself by writing but upon his father's death, he also had a private income to finance his endeavors. When the CCP was attacked in 1927, as recounted above, Mao began his life as an underground revolutionary which continued until the Party's victory in 1949.

Mao's personal life mirrored his political and military struggles. His first wife, Yang Kaihui, was executed by the Nationalist government in 1931. He divorced his second wife and fellow revolutionary, He Zizhen, to marry a young film actress, Jiang Qing, in the late 1930s. Of the ten children born to him as a result of these marriages, only four survived to adulthood and none would gain the stature of their larger-than-life father.

Like Mao, most of the leading figures in the CCP spent their adult lives in the service of the Communist revolution and all boasted special ties to China's top leader. One of the most invaluable men at the top of the Party structure was Zhou Enlai (1898–1976), who became China's Premier and head of the State Council (see description of the State and Party structure, below). Zhou's background was more international and cosmopolitan than Mao's because Zhou studied in Europe as a young man and spoke both French and English. As a result, he brought a broader understanding of international politics and, particularly, of European thinking to the upper echelons of the Party, balancing Mao's China-centered perspective. He had originally joined the Communist movement in Europe, and upon his return to China in 1924, he joined the young Chinese Communist movement based in Shanghai. He barely escaped the 1927 'White Terror' and, like others in the CCP, chose to join Mao at the new base in rural Jiangxi. When Mao rose to the top of the CCP in 1935, Zhou became one of his closest allies. Throughout his long career, he held top posts in both the Party and the government.

During the years of struggle leading to the CCP's victory, the most prominent military figure was Zhu De (1886–1976). Zhu's warlord army origins did not prevent Zhou Enlai from sponsoring him for membership in the CCP. Zhu's arrival at Mao's Jiangxi base in 1928 marked the beginning of a strong alliance between Zhu and Mao which carried the two men through the long war years to victory in 1949. Zhu remained a strong supporter of Mao and held to the principle that the military should always serve the Party, not dominate it.

Another important leader was Liu Shaoqi (1898–1969) who, like Mao, was also from Hunan province in central China. Liu worked as a labor union organizer for the CCP in the 1920s and gained a reputation for both administrative work and theoretical writings. A hero of the Second World War, Liu emerged in 1949 as the number two man in the CCP hierarchy. For a brief period, he was also designated as Mao's heir.

Although somewhat lower on the ladder in 1949, Deng Xiaoping (1904–97) was also among the CCP leaders who joined the movement in his late teens. Educated partly in Europe when he was still in his teens, Deng's youthful experience was closer to that of Zhou Enlai, whom Deng first met while working and studying in Europe. Like Zhou, he returned to join the Chinese movement in 1926 and, following the 1927 purge, joined Mao's Jiangxi forces. Deng survived the Long March, and after the victory in 1949, he was assigned to various regional positions before being brought to Beijing in 1952 as a Deputy Premier under Zhou. His political abilities led to his appointment as Secretary-General of the CCP in 1956, a post which gave him great power and close proximity to the ruling inner circle of the Party. Although Deng was to suffer in the political campaigning initiated by Mao in 1966, he was the ultimate survivor, and emerged as the 'paramount leader' of China in 1978, after Mao's death.

In the early years of the PRC, these men shared a strong personal bond. As a group, they were pragmatic, dedicated, and battle-hardened revolutionaries. Unfortunately, years of experience as professional revolutionaries did not guarantee successful transition to careers that required bureaucratic decision-making and policy formulation in widely diverse areas, such as economic planning, education, medical care, engineering, and technology. Many of the CCP's early errors in attempting too much, too fast may in part be blamed on this old revolutionary guard which forged ahead with little research or caution, embarking on widespread reform without fully comprehending the possible outcomes of their decisions. Regional and county leaders also found their new responsibilities a challenge as the range of decisions for which they were responsible became increasingly complex. Cadres were responsible for everything from initial land reform to lecturing the village population on the new marriage law [*Doc. 1*]. Their limited understanding of these policies was another reason why many of the early efforts to motivate and reform conditions in the rural areas, for example, went more slowly than anticipated and resulted in changes that were not always equitable or effective. It is not surprising, therefore, that many mistakes were made in major policy decisions at the top and in the local level operations of the CCP.

Overall, trained and skilled individuals who were needed to rebuild the country were in short supply in 1949. Less than 1% of the population held college degrees. Many of those with education and/or experience in government positions were former employees of the Nationalist Party and were, therefore, viewed with suspicion. Nonetheless, many former Nationalist officials were retained out of necessity because of the need for educated men and women in positions of responsibility. Likewise, demobilized soldiers were utilized for public works projects as a way of keeping them under the watchful eyes of the new government and its supporters.

THE PARTY, THE GOVERNMENT AND THE MILITARY

The new government emerged in stages. The first constitution was not ready until 1954, a fact which reflected the unexpectedly rapid collapse of Jiang's military in the Civil War. Lacking a formal document as the legal basis of the new state, the CCP organized the Chinese People's Political Consultative Conference (CPPCC), a body which convened in Beijing during September 1949. The 662 delegates to the Conference reflected the CCP's intention to be inclusive and, therefore, included representatives of not only the CCP, which dominated the proceedings, but also a few left-wing members of the Nationalist Party or Guomindang (GMD) and some representatives of pre-Second World War groups like the People's Salvation Association. This body passed the Organic Law of the People's Central Government of the People's Republic of China and the Common Program which served as the provisional legal basis of the new state. In general, the Common Program constituted a plan for gradual change while defending China against 'imperialism, feudalism and bureaucratic capitalism' (Selden, 1979). The Conference named Mao as the new head of state and chose the membership of the Government Council which operated as the central authority in China until the constitution took effect.

Real power, however, lay with the CCP. Mao stood at the top of a vast pyramid that, at its base, included the rank-and-file members of the Party, numbering some 4.5 million in 1949. The Party organization paralleled the civil government, with committees and Party officials at every level, from the village to the Central Government. Party members held government posts as well so that the Party was tightly interwoven with the civil government at all levels in the person of dual office holders. As the CCP's hold strengthened, the two systems became indistinguishable.

A shortage of Party members led to active recruiting in the 1950s. As a result, the Party membership grew to 10 million in 1955. Many of this generation of Party members had rudimentary education at best, but their loyalty to the Party was a more important prerequisite than education. The term *ganbu*, often translated as cadre, referred to both Party and non-Party supporters of the CCP, particularly in the 1950s. In later periods, a cadre was invariably a Party member.

An ambitious cadre could hope to be made head of a local organization in his or her village; smaller numbers achieved posts at the county level and a yet more select group held provincial Party positions. Closer to the seat of power were those with national level posts which constituted the top of the pyramid. In theory, all of these positions were filled by Party elections, but there was, in fact, the most choice at the local level where people usually knew the candidates. For higher posts, the CCP chose candidates who usually stood unopposed.

The top Party leaders were confirmed in their positions by the National Party Congress (NPC), the first of which was held in 1921, the year of the Party's formation. Because of the Second World War, the Party Congress in 1945 was only the Seventh; the Eighth was not convened until 1956. The NPC also elected members of the Central Committee of the CCP, which constituted the top Party elite and numbered from 100 to 300 members. The Central Committee was the real seat of power as its meetings, or plenums, continued year-round whereas the NPC itself met at irregular intervals for only two weeks. More select than the Central Committee was its core group, the Political Bureau, usually abbreviated to Politburo, which included the top 12 to 24 men in China. A final tier was the Standing Committee of the Politburo, which was virtually in permanent session and which thus constituted the ultimate power holders in the country. In the 1950s, Mao dominated this select group.

Mao also dominated the military which, in the 1950s, remained under his close comrade-in-arms, Zhu De. Party supremacy over the military was confirmed by the new government: the civil government included a group called the Central Military Commission, which, technically, was responsible to the National People's Congress. A parallel organization, the Military Affairs Commission, was accountable to the CCP's Central Committee. This dual governmental and Party oversight of the armed forces meant that no military challenge to Mao or the Party emerged in the first two decades of CCP rule.

In terms of its internal organization, the branches of the Chinese military, their division into hierarchal units of command, and their ranks from private to general are the same as those of any modern military. However, as the power behind the Party, the People's Liberation Army (PLA) was not, and is not, politically neutral. Members of the armed forces are trained in communist political theory and every unit has a political officer assigned to it. On several occasions, the PLA was used to support political agendas, as detailed in later chapters, and in this important way it differs considerably from the military establishment in Western states.

In the 1950s, the military played a crucial role in establishing CCP power, particularly in the border regions. Tibet, Xinjiang and Qinghai had become virtually self-governing prior to 1949. The arrival of the PLA in these areas marked the beginning of the reintegration of these areas with the rest of China for the first time in the twentieth century. Between 1950 and 1953, the suppression of 'bandits', a euphemism for any opposition to the CCP as well as for actual criminals, was assigned to the PLA, which gained effective control of the border areas during the first four years of the PRC. ·

INTERNATIONAL RELATIONS AND THE KOREAN WAR

Although many European powers chose to recognize the new government of China in 1949–50, the United States refused to do so. Instead, it officially recognized Jiang's Taiwan government as the legitimate government of China, a decision that would not be reversed until 1979.

With little possibility of economic assistance from Western states, Mao turned to the USSR. In the winter of 1949–50, China's new leader made his first trip beyond China's borders. He visited Moscow to confer with Joseph Stalin and secure Soviet financial assistance for China's reconstruction. Stalin drove a hard bargain. Although the two men signed the Treaty of Alliance and Friendship, the terms required China to repay the US$300 million in aid which was extended as a loan, not a gift. In addition, Stalin secured the rights to explore and develop natural resources in the Xinjiang region, directly across the USSR's far eastern border. The Soviets also retained the use of Dairen and Port Arthur on China's Liaodong peninsula. The agreement also resulted in some 80,000 Chinese going to Russia to study science and technology for various periods of time. An estimated 20,000 Russian and East European experts arrived to assist China in rebuilding heavy industry and other key ventures.

The alliance with the USSR also contributed to China's involvement in the Korean War, which began with the invasion of South Korea by Soviet-backed North Korea in June 1950. Rather than investing Soviet troops in the conflict, Stalin encouraged Mao to protect his eastern flank by assisting the North. As UN troops, about half of whom were American, landed in South Korea, China requested that the United States not intervene. Successive military victories brought the UN troops up the 38th parallel and then across it. China again issued a warning and began to mobilize troops. In November 1950, North Koreans, aided by thousands of Chinese troops, surprised the UN force and drove it all the way back to Seoul. General

MacArthur, in charge of the operation, was recalled in April 1951 and a cease-fire was signed that summer. However, fighting continued until July 1953 when a truce was signed dividing the two Koreas at the same border as before.

The outcome of the Korean War was presented to the Chinese people as a victory, but it came at tremendous cost: between 700,000 and 900,000 Chinese were wounded or killed; scarce resources needed for China's reconstruction were diverted to the war effort; and there were distractions from other programs urgently needing government attention. It also included a personal loss for Mao, whose oldest son, Mao Anying, was killed in the conflict. Casualties for all sides were high: over 160,000 Americans; 520,000 North Koreans; and 400,000 South Koreans.

DOMESTIC POLICY: FIRST STEPS

The first priority was to consolidate control over all of China's territory. While the provinces of China proper were quickly occupied by CCP representatives and PLA units, the extension of CCP rule into the border regions took longer and required the suppression of anti-Communist forces, particularly in the Muslim northwest. Chinese troops also entered Tibetan territory and, as a result, secured an agreement with Tibet's representatives in 1951 [*Docs 2 and 3*]. Mopping-up exercises continued in some areas through 1953, with the strongest resistance coming from the minority peoples of the west and northwest.

Having established itself as the legitimate government of a unified China, the leadership began the implementation of policies in keeping with its mandate for change. Foremost among these was land reform. In 1950, the new government adopted the Agrarian Reform Law; the law itself was of less immediate importance than the fact that the CCP used this initial reform to draw millions of peasant-farmers into the revolutionary process. Rather than simply distribute land to the landless, CCP workers, or cadres, were assigned to villages across China. After identifying the biggest land holders, or landlords, in the village, their task was to organize meetings of the villagers to discuss the 'bitterness' of the past and denounce the landlords as a symbol of the villagers' past oppression. Only after such 'speak bitterness meetings' ended in a verdict on the landlords was the actual land reform carried out. In some instances, landlords judged by the villagers to be exploiters or bullies faced execution; those not considered enemies of the people were denounced and then released with only enough land to support themselves and their families. It is estimated that during the period of the land reform, some 2–3 million landlords were executed by peasant tribunals led by Party representatives. The landlords represented the rural elite, which effectively disappeared in village China, although their children, labeled 'son or daughter of a landlord', continued to bear the stigma of their new class designation. This exercise in class struggle initiated the ordinary peasant into the revolution, closing the door firmly on China's rural, feudal past [*Doc. 4*].

In the land reform movement, approximately half of China's agricultural land was redistributed. The process did not result in equal land holding across China. In the north, where the population was less dense, the average family holdings in the early 1950s was as high as 2.3 acres; in the south, where the population density was very high, a family might have as little as 0.5 of an acre. Nonetheless, this was the first time any modern Chinese government had put the peasant first, and the popularity of the CCP was accordingly high among the rural population in the early years of CCP rule.

Another promise of the CCP was to address the long-standing inequality between men and women. China's old patriarchal order tolerated male dominance of women's lives, encapsulated in the old belief in the 'three obediences' of women: obedience to her father when young; to her husband when married; and to her son in old age. Child marriage, concubinage, and strongly-held views against widow-remarriage all bespoke the low status of women before 1949. The CCP moved quickly in an attempt to rectify these long-standing abuses. The Marriage Law of 1950 [*Doc. 1*] made men and women equal before the law, and proclaimed the right of a woman to seek a divorce from her husband. The legal marriage age for men was set at 20 years and for women at 18 years; no money or financial advantage was allowed either family under the new law and both parties were to marry only by choice, not by coercion or family mandate.

This law proved very controversial. As one observer noted, there were three main obstacles to its implementation: husbands, mothers-in-law, and cadres. Some husbands felt they had the most to lose, as many men had paid money to their bride's family at the time of the marriage and their wives were thus a financial investment as well as mothers of their children and partners in field work. A poor man could have seen the new law as a loss from which he might never recover. Mothers-in-law enjoyed power over daughters-in-law and the new law threatened to upset this long-standing relationship. Finally, cadres found the law troublesome; village leaders feared alienating their neighbors if they pursued implementation of the new regulations too vigorously.

As women learned about their rights under the new law, the divorce rates in some areas rocketed. In response, local cadres often counseled couples to work out their problems. In some instances, the local officials would not grant divorces, especially if family hardship could be proven.

Complaints about the lack of implementation led the Party to renewed efforts to popularize the law in 1953. As the hold of the new government strengthened, the law was more or less enforced with regard to age and other provisions. Still, divorce remained a serious matter and often could be obtained by a woman only after repeated efforts. Women now 'held up half the sky' as Mao once said, but their social standing remained well behind that of men.

Although full equality for women was put on hold, the CCP made advances in other areas. Basic health care was a long-standing need in rural China and the CCP sought to establish clinics in each county and to train health workers to ameliorate the impact of some of the most common diseases. Young people were trained to recognize and report contagious disease and to give talks at the village level on the importance of hygiene and sanitation. The cost was modest; it had to be as China could ill afford to provide health care at anything more than a rudimentary level. The efforts made an impact, for by 1957 life expectancy had risen to 57 years, up from 36 years of age prior to 1949.

Education and literacy constituted another huge challenge to the new government. Literacy programs for adults were begun in many villages, but this task was left to cadres who themselves often lacked much more than basic elementary education. Teachers in their teens were utilized in an effort to increase the people's educational level quickly, and plans were instituted to provide free universal elementary education throughout the country, although by the 1970s this goal had still not been met. The traditional form of Chinese characters was modified by scholars to make the language easier to learn, and gradually the simplified characters became the standard written form. CCP reports of the literacy rates for the 1950s now seem exaggerated, but it is likely that inroads were made, particularly as mass campaigns increasingly used simple slogans, characters for which were plastered on walls in public places all over China.

China's ethnic minorities were also an early subject of CCP concern. Although in terms of percentages, all the minority groups together constituted only 6–7% of China's total population, they were the principal inhabitants of over 60% of China's land (see Map 2). Teams of scholars were assigned the task of studying and identifying groups in order to determine which would receive the official designation of 'national minority'. Over 400 groups petitioned the government for recognition, but the government initially only designated 40 groups as official minorities. The number eventually reached 55 where it has remained. The CCP's goal was to grant the most populous of the groups a certain amount of autonomy in their traditional homelands. These included the Tibetans, Mongols, and Hmong (known as Miao in China) as well as peoples less well known in the West, such as the 6 million Uighurs, a Turkic Muslim group in the far northwest. Much less numerous minorities like the Ewenki, the Hani, and the Lisu (see Table 1 for a partial list of minorities) also received autonomy, although the administrative unit was the county rather than the province or region level [*Doc. 5*].

Table 1   Minority populations in the People's Republic of China

Minority nationalities with populations over one million in 1990

Name	Population	Location
Bai	1,594,827	Yunnan
Buyi	2,545,059	Guizhou
Dai [Thai]	1,025,128	Yunnan
Dong	2,514,014	Guizhou
Hani	1,253,952	Yunnan
Hui	8,602,978	Nationwide
Kazakh	1,111,718	Xinjiang
Korean	1,920,597	North-eastern provinces
Li	1,110,900	Yunnan
Manchu	9,821,180	North-eastern provinces
Miao [Hmong]	7,398,035	South-eastern provinces
Mongolian	4,806,849	Inner Mongolia
Tibetan	4,593,330	Tibet, Qinghai, Sichuan
Tujia	5,704,223	Hunan
Uyghur	7,214,431	Xinjiang
Yao	2,134,013	Southern provinces, Hainan
Yi	6,572,173	South and south-western provinces
Zhuang	15,489,630	Guangxi

Minority populations under one million in 1990

Name	Population	Location
Daur	121,357	North-east, Xinjiang
Dongxiang	373,872	Gansu
Ewen [Ewenki]	26,315	North-eastern provinces
Gelao	437,997	Guizhou
Jingbo	119,209	Yunnan
Kyrgyz [Kirghiz]	141,549	Xinjiang
Lahu	411,476	Yunnan
Lisu	574,856	Yunnan
Maoan	71,968	Guangxi
Mulao	159,328	Guangxi
Naxi	78,009	Yunnan
Nu	27,123	Yunnan
Pumi	29,657	Yunnan
Qiang	198,252	Sichuan
Salar	87,697	Gansu
She	630,378	Fujian
Shui	345,993	Guizhou
Tadjik	33,538	Western Xinjiang

Name	Population	Location
Tu	191,624	Qinghai
Wa	351,974	Yunnan
Xibo	172,847	Xinjiang
14 additional groups with populations of less than 25,000		
Total Minority Population	91,200,314	
Han Chinese Population	1,042,482,187	
Total Population	1,224,882,815	

Source: Adapted from Renmin Ribao [People's Daily], 14 November 1991, p. 3, and Gladney (1998).

The regional autonomy system which was established in the 1950s was intended to offset the fact that, unlike the USSR, the new state did not allow any part of China to secede. As part of the new system, the Central Government announced plans to assist minority regions to advance. Although relatively little could be done toward this goal in the 1950s, the system held out the promise of financial support and a measure of local control over affairs to peoples who had been neglected or ignored by previous governments.

Hundreds of miles away from the minority areas, in urban China, the goal was to nationalize all privately-held businesses and industries. In the initial phase, the new government bought a number of enterprises from their owners, some of whom remained as managers or supervisors. Managerial staff was retained at major industries and manufacturing plants. Slowly, China's urban business centers resumed production. Cities were cleaned of crime and vice, with brothels, gaming houses and drug traffickers put out of business. The new austerity of city-life made it clear that the old order was, indeed, now gone.

The above policies were presented to the people through mass campaigns, led by local cadres whose job was to explain things at a level the peasants, many of whom were poorly educated or illiterate, could understand. The visionary goal of the Party leadership was to create a new socialist person who would see his or her loyalties as being first to the Party and the state and then to the family. A selfless altruism was required to buoy the country and carry socialism to its final goal – the creation of a true paradise where all would be equal and all needs would be met.

Mass campaigns not only fostered patriotism and loyalty; they were also used to teach people the new, revolutionary vocabulary of the PRC. Individuals who did not embrace the new ideas of relations between men and women, for instance, were called 'Old Feudals'. Oppression and its cause – the capitalist economic system – was taught to everyone through the political campaigns as well as in the schools. With the new vocabulary came popularization of the simplified Chinese characters that conveyed the new ideas, providing political lessons along with basic literacy.

Some campaigns aimed at fostering political ideas, but others were more pragmatic. The 'Four Pests Campaign', for example, called upon people to kill the four most common pests – flies, mosquitos, sparrows and rats. The populace embraced this campaign with enthusiasm but, like some other early policies, it was not well thought-out. With the sparrow population diminished as a result of vigorous pursuit, many insects lost a natural predator and multiplied enormously, threatening crops. Still, the elimination of the other three pests may have contributed to somewhat better health statistics for the 1950s.

With these and other fundamental changes underway, the CCP turned to the larger issue of moving China toward a socialist economy. By the mid-1950s, the government had assumed total control of all enterprises. Growth in agricultural output had initially been strong as farmers relished their new land-holding status. The organization of cooperative groups among villagers, called Mutual Aid Teams, encouraged families to pool their tools and equipment. This step had been relatively successful, as many families who lacked basic equipment could now share the labor of a neighbor's water buffalo or plough to enhance their productivity. However, as the local cadres pushed farmers to pool their newly acquired land as well, forming larger, more efficiently farmed plots, resentments emerged. In 1955, only 14% of the peasants had joined the new units, called lower-level Agricultural Producers Cooperatives (APCs). That summer the CCP was faced with a decision about the future of agricultural policy: should it move ahead more quickly toward a fully collectivized rural economy or give farmers time to adjust to the changes which had so recently occurred? Mao's decision was to move ahead more quickly. His impatience with gradual change and a more cautious approach pushed the Party leadership toward rapid change. By the end of 1955, almost all peasant-farmers were enrolled in some form of APC; the following year, rural China was dominated by the higher form of APC. The new APC system required that peasants not only share tools and equipment, but also pool all their land. Each individual therefore began to work for the state rather than for him or herself, receiving wages based on the amount of labor, tools, land and equipment given to the APC. Faced with little alternative, however, peasants joined the new APCs reluctantly; as a result, rather than increasing output, agricultural production reached lower than anticipated levels in 1956 and 1957. Thus the CCP once more grappled with the issue of the pace of reforms.

Mao himself wanted faster change. Nonetheless, in 1956 he called upon CCP cadres to offer their comments and criticism. Initially, none stepped forward. Mao's stature as the head of the Party and the State was so great that any criticism of his policies was, for many loyal Party members, deemed disrespectful if not outright counter to the revolution's goals. Only after repeated urgings from Mao himself did criticism emerge in the spring of 1957. Called the '100 Flowers Campaign', the movement derived its name from a classical Chinese phrase: 'Let one hundred flowers bloom, let one hundred schools of thought contend.' The goal was to have widespread discussion as a precursor to the major push toward a socialist economy, ostensibly as a way to identify and then rectify shortcomings in policy implementation.

At first, comments were relatively mild, but the number and the critical nature of the solicited remarks quickly grew as Party cadres urged members to speak up. People in and outside the Party reported abuses of cadre power, including bullying and forced compliance with directives. Minority cadres faced accusations of mistreating their own people in the border regions; intellectuals complained about the state of education and the plight of students. Looked at dispassionately, the critique of the Party offered in the spring 1957 was hardly surprising given the enormous tasks at hand and the still evolving Party apparatus which relied on poorly trained local leaders and incomplete and/or inaccurate statistics for its economic planning. Nor should it have been surprising to the leadership that policy to date still faced numerous major and minor problems at all levels. In May and early June 1957, criticism continued to flow toward the center at Beijing.

A week into June, Mao and the Central Committee called a halt to the campaign. To the consternation of many loyal CCP members, the Party announced that counter-revolutionaries within the country had used the opportunity of the 100 Flowers Campaign to vilify the Party and its policies. The sharpest critics were detained and many individuals found themselves accused of being 'rightist' and against the Party [*Doc. 6*]. A new 'Anti-rightist Campaign' unfolded, and thousands of hapless CCP members found themselves sent into the rural areas for re-education at the hands of the peasant population. Their compliance with Party directions to offer a critique of the Party's methods and policies only brought what many must have seen as unwarranted retribution. Many cadres began years of labor at tasks such as raising pigs or planting crops. Some used the opportunity for reflection on the revolution and its goals, but others simply suffered the penalty assigned by the Party, hoping that in time the 'rightist' label would be lifted.

Having effectively silenced all real and potential critics, Mao moved forward with plans for the rapid shift of all China to the commune system. An opportunity for open discussion and realistic appraisal of the Party's achievements was lost. Instead, Mao announced that China would now begin a 'great leap forward' in order to catch up with European powers like Britain in just 15 years. What was to become the first great cataclysm to hit the PRC was thus launched by Mao and his supporters in 1958.

CHAPTER FOUR

THE RADICAL MAOIST PHASE, 1958–76

By 1958, eight years had passed since Mao declared the People's Republic. Mao himself was now 63. He had reason to be pleased with China's progress since the victory in 1949. China's agricultural production had returned to pre-Second World War levels, and the average life expectancy in China had reached 57 years of age. Modest improvements in health care and education augured well for the future. Technical assistance from the USSR had boosted China's industrial production as the 'lean to one side' policy bore fruit, although the Chinese relationship with the new Soviet leader, Khrushchev, was already severely strained. The international community saw China confront the United States and UN troops in Korea, and its stature among other developing states had increased as a result.

As the leadership assessed its overall position and weighed the impact of the 'rightist' element it believed had infiltrated the Party at various levels, Mao declared that the time had come to forge ahead rather than allow the Party to rest on its accomplishments. In the summer of 1958, China embarked on the Great Leap Forward, an ambitious economic plan to modernize all aspects of China's production capacity.

To this end, all peasants were organized into rural communes in a matter of months. Huge in size, the 24,000 communes superceded the county-level governments as political structures. The new centralized economy called for the assignment of quotas to each commune. The State would collect a percentage from each commune while the remainder would sustain the commune members. Each individual became part of a smaller work unit, called a brigade, which in actual practice was often a reconstituted form of the village. Brigades were given work assignments and each member was paid in work points. These were tallied at year's end based on the amount of work done. Individuals then used work points in the commune stores for cloth, manufactured items and other goods; some families also received part payment in cash.

The single most important and enduring change brought about by the Great Leap Forward was the entry of women into the work force. The new system required more full-time workers and peasant women were the answer. Women had always worked in the fields in some parts of China, but their work was often sporadic and seasonal because of their primary role in caring for children and running the household. In 1958, women began to work full-time in the fields. The average number of work points paid to a woman was lower than the rates paid to men, but with women's wages regularized, their financial contribution to the family was recognized as important. To free them from household chores, commune canteens fed the workers, sometimes offering as many as five meals a day and freeing women from this time-consuming task. Commune nurseries took over the care of infants and toddlers, and schools assumed daily care of children of school age. Chinese women became an integral part of the country's work force, although it would still be some years before the principle of equal pay for equal work was embraced in rural and urban settings.

Mao's vision included the eventual self-reliance of each individual commune. Thus, ideally, each commune would have its own education and medical system, its own diverse agricultural production, as well as its own industries. Despite the illogic of requiring each commune to produce goods for which it had no locally available resources, the new campaign called upon commune members to embrace self-sufficiency by producing their own basic necessities, including iron.

The production of iron and steel consumed the energies of millions of Chinese peasants. They collected anything made of iron, from nails to cooking pots, and melted them down. To fuel the greedy, home-made furnaces, some communes denuded the landscape of trees and brush, at a huge environmental cost. The home-made furnaces also absorbed countless hours of labor as men and women tended the inefficient furnaces night and day. As an exercise in heightening revolutionary ardor, the push to make iron may have been a temporary success; however, the end product was tons of quite un-useable metal.

Ignorance also led many communes into agricultural disaster. Cadres ignorant about the rudiments of agriculture advised on planting techniques and, in many instances, proposed impossibly high quotas that were intended to please their superiors and demonstrate enthusiasm for the new system. Intent on surpassing their quotas, some commune officials resorted to stratagems such as ordering the farmers to plant crops close together or to spread seed, or fertilizer, in thick layers, believing this would lead to enormous crops. The predictable result was that young plants had no space to grow and died before reaching maturity. The combination of peasant reluctance to criticize or challenge authority combined with over-zealous cadres' misguided advice contributed to a growing crisis in the countryside [Doc. 7].

The government-controlled media reported great increases in grain production. Based on inflated figures reported to the government by commune officials, the State took its mandated percentage of crops in tax. But because the actual amount of grain harvested was in reality lower, the amount collected by the State was a far larger percentage in real terms. As food supplies on the communes dwindled, grain and foodstuffs collected by the government rotted in warehouses.

By the spring of 1959, China faced food shortages. In sharp contrast to the reports of bumper harvests, urban residents found little food in the market. Rural China experienced acute shortfalls, but with travel in China restricted, the real dimensions of the crisis were not widely known except among higher Party officials. In July 1959, the Central Committee gathered at Lushan, in Shandong province, to assess the situation. The only outspoken critic was Peng Dehuai, a Long March survivor and admired military leader. His letter to Mao on the situation in the rural areas, which he personally had visited, indicated grave problems in policy implementation and outcomes, as well as growing food shortages [*Doc. 8*]. Although the tone of his letter was quite mild, it criticized the Great Leap and its chief architect, Mao himself. Mao's anger at Peng became public: the offending letter was copied and circulated to 150 top members of the CCP, and Mao demanded that Peng and his letter be repudiated. With no one in the leadership daring to counter Mao, Peng was effectively silenced, as were any other would-be critics.

A year before the meeting at Lushan, Mao had already decided he would step down from the position of head of state (President), a largely ceremonial position. At the Lushan Conference, the CCP accepted Mao's formal resignation from that position, although an attempt was made to divorce this move from the difficulties arising from the Great Leap – the worst of which was yet to come. Nonetheless, his resignation and subsequent shift away from the day-to-day workings of the government suggested Mao's tacit acceptance of responsibility for the deficiencies of the Great Leap. Liu Shaoqi, long regarded as Mao's successor, assumed the Presidency in 1959.

That summer, the inflated reports of bumper harvests continued, as did the foolhardy new planting methods, some of which were personally espoused by Mao. The result was deepening crisis. Crops that year failed, as they did in 1960 and 1961. Chinese came to refer to these as the 'Three Bitter Years' for the impact on rural China was devastating. The very young and very old died first, but even the able-bodied weakened as a result of the severe shortages. An estimated 30 million Chinese died before the country began to recover (Becker, 1996). Peasants were forbidden to leave their communes and, as a result, millions of Chinese remained unaware of the widespread impact of the Chairman's Great Leap.

During this terrible time, Mao withdrew from politics and became increasingly isolated. He devoted himself to writing and to reading China's great classic literature. Liu and other top leaders were left to deal with the disastrous aftermath of his policy.

Liu was in an awkward position, given the fact that Mao's stature and position as Chairman of the CCP still gave him precedence over all other Party figures. After 1959, it was up to Liu and others in the government to salvage Chinese agriculture and mitigate the disaster. One step was to allow private plots so that farmers could augment their families' diet from their own individual gardens after completing their work for the commune. Bonuses and other incentives rewarded the most diligent. Administratively, Liu divided the huge, unwieldy communes into smaller, more manageable units. The number of communes thus grew to over 70,000. Food and cloth were rationed in an effort to stretch resources. Factory and industrial workers also saw their bonuses and incentives restored in an effort to boost production. Slowly, China began to recover. Production levels rose once more as the resilient peasants and workers rescued the country from poor central planning.

TIBET

As mentioned earlier, following the victory of the PLA in 1949 and the establishment of the new government, Chinese military units moved to occupy Tibet and, from a position of military strength, signed an agreement with representatives of the young Dalai Lama, the temporal and spiritual ruler of Tibet. Part of that agreement assured the Tibetans that no socialist land reform would be carried out in Tibetan territory [*Doc. 2*]. The CCP kept their promise, but their re-organization of provincial boundaries resulted in many Tibetans living outside the new Tibetan borders. Tibetans who now found themselves residents of the Chinese province of Sichuan were required to participate in land reform like their Han neighbors. When local authorities moved to enforce the land reforms, Tibetan resistance became violent and open fighting erupted in late 1955. As a result of the fighting in Sichuan, Tibetans fled to Lhasa, demanding both protection and action from the Tibetan government which they expected to uphold what they saw as their right to retain their personal land holdings. But with little military strength available to assert his people's claims, the Dalai Lama sought to calm the situation and solicit support from outside as a counter to Chinese strength.

The situation remained tense, continuing into 1957. Mao himself assured the Dalai Lama that he would delay land reform in China for another six years and possibly longer. Unimpressed with Chinese assurances, however, factions within Tibet began arming themselves, some with assistance from the United States (Goldstein, 1997). The situation was brought to a head in March 1959 when Tibetan leaders decided that the

Dalai Lama would only be safe outside Tibet. He and his top advisers fled to India under cover of darkness. A bloody uprising against Chinese rule erupted but was quickly suppressed. From exile in India, the Dalai Lama declared the 17-Point Agreement invalid, as did the Chinese government.

Once fully in control of the region, the CCP and the PLA subjected the region to intense campaigns aimed at breaking the power of the religious elite. Monasteries that engaged in any form of resistance were destroyed and the monks forced to return to secular lives. A massive propaganda campaign denounced the old feudal society of traditional Tibet. From the CCP perspective, the Tibetans were now liberated and free to travel the socialist road. From the viewpoint of many Tibetans, however, the year 1959 marked the beginning of Chinese efforts to obliterate their culture and religion [*Doc. 3*].

THE SINO-SOVIET SPLIT

The situation in Tibet and the growing problems stemming from the Great Leap were only two of several serious issues confronting China in 1959. Mao's growing disagreement with the new Soviet leader, Khrushchev, who was pursuing a policy of peaceful coexistence with the United States, now deepened. In addition to the policy toward capitalist states, Khrushchev also asked for concessions from China, such as the right to build a radio station in China and to re-fuel ships in China, all of which were rejected by Mao in 1959. Mao also believed that Peng Dehuai's criticisms of the Great Leap had been influenced by the USSR.

By 1960, the growing divide was an open split, and that summer the USSR ordered Russian advisers in China home. From that time onwards, the two communist powers' interaction was marked by varying degrees of hostility. Not until 1989 was a Soviet leader welcomed in China.

THE SEEDS OF THE CULTURAL REVOLUTION

Having stepped down as head of state in 1959, Mao played a decreasing role in the work of the government. He was no longer as visible as he had been, and was less available to old friends or even formerly close advisers. He became a remote and distant figure, although he continued to live near other top leaders in Zhongnanhai, a guarded compound next to the old imperial palace in the center of Beijing. His third wife, Jiang Qing, lived in the compound in separate quarters, as did Mao's daughter by his second wife, He Zizhen, and his daughter by Jiang Qing. Later, his family circle expanded to include a nephew, Mao Yuanmin.

During this hiatus, Mao became increasingly disturbed by the efforts of the Party leadership to resurrect the battered Chinese economy. Rather than carrying the goals of the revolution forward, he came to believe that the Party was straying off the socialist path. Behind the compound walls, Mao conceived a new campaign to prevent the de-railing of the revolution and to ensure a new generation of revolutionary successors from among those coming of age in 'New China'. Called the 'Socialist Education Campaign', the goal of this new mass movement was to rekindle revolutionary fervor.

With China finally recovering from the Great Leap, Mao's new campaign was launched in 1962. Workers and farmers studied Mao's works and attended rallies and meetings. All were exhorted to apply Mao's words and many dutifully attempted to do so. Whether the masses reciting slogans could be entrusted with the future of the revolution, however, remained an open question. Mao himself was clearly not satisfied with the way in which the campaign was carried out and increasingly questioned the commitment of the Liu government to the revolution as he envisioned it. The lackluster campaign, the emergence of what Mao saw as capitalist tendencies in a system which offered bonuses and other incentives for workers, and his own increasing distance from the daily routines of government business all contributed to Mao's dissatisfaction with the political climate of the early 1960s.

The situation created opportunities for some within the Party who sought to bolster their own position through zealous support of Mao as the country's 'Great Helmsman'. Minister of Defense Lin Biao catered to the image of Mao as supreme leader by publishing a book, *Quotations of Chairman Mao*, later popularly referred to as the 'Little Red Book' because of the bright red plastic that covered the pocket-sized volumes. Everyone in the military was required to read and memorize the quotes. Under Lin's direction, the PLA became a stronghold of Maoist teachings [*Doc. 9*].

Others, particularly intellectuals within the Party, saw in the changed atmosphere an opportunity to critique Mao. Although none would openly accuse Mao of making mistakes, more subtle means could be found. One such means was the publication of a play, *Hai Rui Dismissed from Office*. The author was a well-known intellectual, Wu Han, who enjoyed strong ties to influential members of the CCP, including the President, Liu Shaoqi, and the CCP General Secretary, Deng Xiaoping. Wu also served as deputy mayor of Beijing, under Mayor Peng Zhen. Ostensibly, his play was about a loyal official of the Ming period who was wrongfully dismissed for telling the emperor the truth. The parallel with Mao's dismissal of Peng Dehuai, the most outspoken critic of Mao's Great Leap, was hard to miss. In 1965, Mao decided to act. In what some scholars view as the opening volley of Mao's last great political campaign, the Cultural Revolution, Mao ordered a critique of Wu Han's play, but compliance was repeatedly delayed, much to Mao's annoyance. Finally, spurred on by repeated urgings from his wife, Jiang Qing, Mao had a critical review published in Shanghai. Mayor Peng

Zhen, who had managed to protect Wu Han for a time by asserting that the play was 'only' literature, could no longer do so.

By the spring of 1966, Mao and his closest supporters had won. Mao, aided by his wife and her leftist supporters, prepared to launch the last great campaign of his life.

THE GREAT PROLETARIAN CULTURAL REVOLUTION

At the age of 72, Mao initiated what became a violent and destructive campaign that set Party member against Party member and generation against generation. All across China, violent confrontation marked this effort to destroy, once and for all, the old society, and replace it with a new, socialist order led by the generation born and raised under the communist system. This new generation of 'revolutionary successors' became the vanguard of the new radical campaign led by Mao and his wife.

In August 1966, the CCP's Central Committee, under the direct leadership of a newly energized and publicly visible Mao, issued a directive calling for a great 'cultural revolution' to begin [*Doc. 10*]. The directive called for an open attack on all remnants of the old society so that a new, truly revolutionary society could emerge. The call to destroy the 'Four Olds' resonated among young people in ways that even Mao must have found unexpectedly powerful.

To jump-start the new movement, young people were directed to form revolutionary groups called Red Guards. All over China, young people answered this call. To impress upon them the importance of their task as the leaders of the new movement, Red Guards were invited to come to Beijing where they could catch a glimpse of the Chairman as he greeted massed audiences in Tiananmen Square. The frenzied gatherings stirred young people who vowed their undying loyalty to the Chairman. The cult of Mao, fostered by Lin Biao and other radical leftists, swept across China as thousands of young people converged on Beijing to see their hero. Far from being spontaneous occasions, however, the marshaling of large numbers of Red Guards in the Square and their movement in and out of Beijing was orchestrated by the military and radical factions in the Party. The young revolutionaries would spend the night in quarters arranged for their temporary use and would then be quickly sent on their way out of the city so that new arrivals could be accommodated.

Many of the young people who flocked to Beijing in 1966 saw themselves as saving China from the burdens of the oppressive past and upholding the truth of Mao Zedong Thought. They carried their 'Little Red Books' as a sign of their devotion and sported 'Mao badges' of all shapes and sizes which they pinned to their shirts and jackets.

Honored by Mao's call to action, the youngsters began their onslaught on traditional Chinese culture. Teenage leaders spouting Party slogans and rhetoric attacked their designated targets of 'old culture, old ideas, old customs and old habits' with great enthusiasm. Elderly Chinese who had kept clothing or objects from the past were subjected to lectures and harangues by youngsters who burst into houses and apartments at will to search for any goods from the 'old' categories. Some items were taken away, others were smashed, destroyed or burned with great fanfare out in the street.

Not only mementos and heirlooms suffered Red Guard attentions. Party leaders, teachers, and professors found themselves under attack for any casual remark that suggested disrespect to Chairman Mao or the CCP. Students whose parents wore the 'rightist cap' as a result of previous campaigns, or those with relatives in Taiwan or Hong Kong, were singled out for abuse by their class mates. Terror descended for both Party loyalists and anyone formerly given a 'black' label as the hunt for supposed counter-revolutionaries spread across China [*Doc. 11*].

The Red Guards did not constitute a single entity. Initially, children of Party cadres took the lead in organizing Red Guard groups; children of the 'black' categories, such as those from landlord families, were not allowed to join. In the autumn of 1966, however, the Party lifted restrictions on who could join the Red Guard movement and the number of groups proliferated. Youngsters whose background had excluded them could now also demonstrate their loyalty to Mao. Like others from politically acceptable categories, they, too, danced the loyalty dance and confessed all their innermost thoughts to China's Great Helmsman, Chairman Mao. All chose names for their local groups that reflected their loyalty to Mao, such as 'Protectors of Mao Zedong Thought Red Guards' or 'August First Red Guards'.

As fervor grew in 1966, the Party continued to facilitate the movement of young people around the country. Any young person with an armband declaring him or her to be a Red Guard (*Hongweibing*) could board a train for Beijing or Shanghai, or other 'revolutionary' destinations. Remembering those days years later, many participants noted that they had never known such freedom. Thousands took advantage of the sudden opportunity to see places they had never dreamed of visiting. Troops of young people formed their own 'Long March' contingents to 'gain revolutionary experience' as the Party exhorted them to do, and marched on foot along routes where Mao and the PLA had fought for the revolution.

Throughout the course of the Cultural Revolution period, some young students simply followed their own local leaders and many did little more than chant slogans and turn up for rallies (Jiang and Ashley, 2000). A minority proved zealous participants, attacking any adult, regardless of social status, who was deemed by them to be anti-Maoist. Beatings and humiliating parades through the streets awaited some victims; less fortunate targets died at the hands of China's young in the name of Mao's revolution.

Girls and women became equal participants in the movement, leading their own Red Guard bands, traveling on the trains 'to make revolution', and in some instances leading or participating in attacks on hapless victims of the movement. As daughters of the revolution, they wore the same pseudo-military clothes as the male participants, and chanted the same aggressive slogans. It appeared that this new generation of young Chinese women were fully enfranchised members of the new order.

Mao used the opportunity of widening chaos to attack his own chosen targets. Liu Shaoqi and his wife, Wang Guangmei, both became victims. Liu disappeared by the end of 1966; he died in 1969 as a result of his persecution. His wife was vilified before a huge crowd in Beijing and then sentenced to years of solitary confinement in Beijing's prison system. Another major target proved to be Deng Xiaoping who was attacked as the country's 'number one capitalist roader', an unlikely epithet for a man who had, since his teens, been dedicated to the socialist cause. Nonetheless, he, too, disappeared. Although he and his family suffered during the most virulent phase of the Cultural Revolution, he re-emerged in 1973 (see discussion in the next chapter) and was later restored to his position on the Politburo.

In 1968, competing groups of Red Guards began to fight among themselves, with each group declaring itself the true protector of the Chinese revolution and Mao Zedong Thought. Former and active members of the PLA joined forces with student groups, increasing the level of violence. Stones and bricks gave way to guns. In pitched battles both sides suffered casualties; thousands died in fighting between army units ordered to restore calm and armed student groups intent on victory for their own Red Guard faction. Some of the worst fighting occurred in the western province of Sichuan and in the central China city of Wuhan. By 1969, competing Red Guard groups closed businesses and disrupted transport and distribution of food and goods in towns and cities all over China.

That same year, in the northwestern Muslim region of Xinjiang, a brief shooting war broke out between units of the USSR and the PLA on the Sino-Soviet border. This threat to the nation's security led the CCP to announce an end to the Cultural Revolution in Xinjiang. That summer, Mao decided that the movement had reached its objectives and declared victory over counter-revolutionary forces. Officially, the movement was over. But while the military quickly ended Red Guard activities in Xinjiang, stopping the chaos elsewhere took more time.

To curtail Red Guard activities, the CCP ordered young people to return home. When students on some urban university campuses continued to hold rallies and fight, the PLA was sent in to stop them. Arrests eliminated the most outspoken supporters of the movement and a harsh crackdown brought quiet to the campuses at last. To limit young activists further, hundreds of young people were sent down to the rural areas to work on communes and on huge state construction projects. The harsh conditions and poor diet quickly drained youthful energies as manual labor replaced political rallies (Jiang and Ashley, 2000). By the summer's end calm was returning to China. Mao declared the movement a success, but how he measured that success was not immediately apparent, even to Party stalwarts.

In 1969, Mao was again the most powerful man in China. His views on the need for maintaining revolutionary zeal and guarding against all enemies who would dare impede the progress of the country toward socialism seemed unchallengeable. To prevent a return of the bureaucratic style of those now condemned as 'taking the capitalist road', Mao called for a new kind of government organization. Former titles and positions disappeared; in their place were Revolutionary Committees which now ran governments, communes and industries. Typically, these included a worker, a cadre, and a member of the PLA. Leaders of many provinces and regions had disappeared in the Cultural Revolution, replaced by men and women loyal to the goals of Mao's new radical agenda. With China's culture now supposedly revolutionized and remnants of the feudal past destroyed, or at least badly damaged, the Party hierarchy turned inward to continue the struggle for power behind closed doors once more.

The violent phase of the Cultural Revolution, from 1966 to 1969, deeply marked Chinese society. In addition to the estimated half a million people who died from torture, beatings and forced suicide, thousands more were brutalized as a result of the frenzied activities of Red Guard factions who inflicted untold physical and psychological damage. Young people raised without the supervision of parents who had been sent away for re-education lived hand to mouth on the fringes of society. Those whose elders returned from years of hard labor witnessed the enormous physical and psychological toll, from which some never recovered. Many young people who inflicted the humiliating verbal abuse and public beatings on neighbors and former teachers in the name of the revolution would later hear the CCP's apology to some of their victims, leaving the former Red Guards to reflect on why they had been urged to commit such outrages on people who were now deemed to be innocent of all charges against them. For a whole generation, the realization that their loyalties earned them only manual labor jobs in rural China and that their supposed 'counter-revolutionary' targets were exonerated contributed to changing attitudes toward the Party and its ageing leadership.

Economically, the country also suffered. Because the major struggles were in urban areas, production fell as workers spent their time in political struggle. Agricultural production in many areas also dropped, and income stagnated. One of the few positive developments was that the urban turmoil brought opportunities for small town and village enterprises, which produced necessities like chemical fertilizer and small consumer goods that city factories, absorbed with political activity, failed to supply. Overall, however, Mao's plans for a strong economic and military state in his own lifetime suffered yet another major setback as the Cultural Revolution finally drew to a close.

All of this generated a new cynicism about the CCP and Mao's revolution. Because the times required it, ordinary Chinese became adept at attending meetings and saying little; at hiding all real feelings and guessing what the local leadership wanted them to say and do. 'Politically correct' slogans and jargon were the order of the day. Even formerly stalwart members re-examined their long-held views. Although the majority of the people who suffered during the movement were ultimately rehabilitated and re-admitted to the Party ranks, the cynicism remained [*Doc. 12*].

Even the return to some semblance of normal life after 1969 was shattered in 1971 for many Chinese with the amazing announcement that Mao's designated successor, Minister of Defense Lin Biao, had attempted to assassinate Mao. In what came to be called the '571 Affair' China's official press reported that Lin and his family had plotted to blow up Mao's house, killing him and his entourage. When the plan failed, largely as a result of Lin's own daughter informing the Party of her father's plans, the Chinese news media reported that Lin had been shot down in an aeroplane flown by his son, an officer in the Air Force. A photograph of the crash site somewhere in Mongolia purported to show the remains of the plane, but the 'official' picture revealed little more than burned wreckage in an unidentifiable locale.

Party members and former Red Guards heard this news with a sense of shock. The infallible Mao had personally chosen Lin. How could he have made such an enormous mistake – trusting a man who could plot his death? People who had been taught that every word Mao uttered was true, now had to confront the fact that Mao was, after all, only human. Despite the jolt to the Party faithful delivered by the revelation of Lin's plot, Mao remained at the pinnacle of CCP power – he was too commanding a figure and, furthermore, his radical supporters appeared to hold firmly to power at every level in the country. Those who no longer respected their ailing leader's decisions now bided their time as Mao's health began to deteriorate.

Then, in 1972, came another surprising piece of news: China would host the American President, Richard Nixon. Mao and Nixon represented polar opposites. Mao presented himself and China as the only true Communist movement and continued to denounce the USSR, just as it denounced American imperialist intentions and its capitalist system. Equally committed at the other end of the spectrum, Nixon held strongly anti-Communist views. Nonetheless, both men considered other internal and international factors in making an about-face and agreeing to meet. Nixon's decision was not the result of any great foresight or political acuity, as is suggested by many American sources, but instead was a result of shifting power relations within the international community. For over two decades, the United States endorsed the fiction of Taiwan's Nationalist Party, still under the leadership of the defeated Jiang Jieshi, as the sole legitimate government of China. This fiction was wearing thin as China continued to gain support among the world's nations for its admittance to the United Nations. Year by year the vote to admit China and oust Taiwan from the UN and from its US-backed seat on the Security Council shifted toward China. By 1971, it was clear that the United States would soon lose the vote over Taiwan. Nixon simply read the extremely large writing on the wall. Of necessity, the United States had to begin talks with China. Rather than allow this to look like a defeat for his administration, Nixon turned the tables and presented his visit to China as a breakthrough in international relations. Clearly, it would only be a matter of time before the United States recognized the PRC as China's legitimate government.

For Mao, the menace of the USSR was paramount. The 1969 fighting on the western border led to military build-up on both sides, but other borders also had to be guarded. The USSR remained an ally of North Korea on China's northeast border and, in the south, was allied to North Viet Nam. Further, relations with India were also strained during the Cultural Revolution, constituting yet another sensitive strip of border. China, therefore, could benefit from improved relations with the United States, however slight that improvement might be.

Go-betweens arranged the talks. In February 1972, the two sides met in Beijing, where Nixon received a muted public reception. Most of the Chinese residents of the capital city were not aware of the American president's visit, although it was extensively and ecstatically reported in the American and world press. The results of the exchange between Mao and Nixon were encapsulated in the Shanghai Communiqué which called for continued talks and movement toward normalization of Sino-American relations. Although such normalization would not come until 1979, the Nixon visit signaled a new era in Sino-American relations.

After the Nixon visit, Mao's various illnesses continued their assault on his health: Parkinson's disease, heart disease, and other maladies weakened the leader. Other elderly comrades-in-arms also battled illness. The first to succumb was Zhou Enlai, who died of cancer in January 1976. A great outpouring of national grief met the news of his death. A few months later, Mao's longtime military commander, Zhu De, also died. The dragon year of

1976 was also Mao's last: he died on 9 September 1976, leaving as his most important legacy a unified state – achieved at a great cost to millions of his countrymen.

The nation now waited to learn who would succeed Mao. In October, the startling news came that Mao's widow, Jiang Qing, and her three closest supporters in the Cultural Revolution had been arrested. In the Chinese press, the group was called 'The Gang of Four' and together stood accused of crimes against the State. A further surprise was the announcement that a relatively unknown Party member, Hua Guofeng, would now lead China into the post-Mao era.

ASSESSING MAO'S IMPACT ON CHINA

Over a quarter of a century after his death, the image of Mao is once again an important symbol of the Chinese people's struggle for national unity and pride. Despite his legacy of the disastrous Great Leap Forward and the chaotic Cultural Revolution, Mao remains an icon for many Chinese, who honor him as China's greatest twentieth-century leader. Beyond China's borders, however, he is portrayed negatively – as a tyrant and a dictator. His Western biographers (Spence, 1999; Terrill, 1993) reserve their praise for his pre-1949 role as a revolutionary leader who unified and strengthened China after years of devastating warfare.

Any assessment of Mao must take into account his whole career, both before and after 1949. Clearly, his career as a revolutionary is inseparable from the period of dramatic changes that marked his adult life prior to 1949. Better than any other leader of his day, Mao understood how great the need was for fundamental change in the countryside. But he also believed he had discovered the means to bring about that change – through leadership of the majority of the Chinese population, the peasant-farmers in China's vast countryside. To coalesce the power of the peasantry, Mao tapped into traditional views of authority and government that included loyalty and self-sacrifice as central values. To sway students and intellectuals, communism was presented as a set of modern scientific principles that could resolve China's seemingly insurmountable problems. China's heightened sense of nationalism and unified efforts to fight Japan during the Second World War were also explicitly harnessed by Mao and the CCP to expand their appeal. By the end of the war, Mao and the CCP emerged with a strong following in northern China that laid the foundation for their 1949 victory over Jiang and his forces. The great feat of wresting control from the GMD and the creation of a strong, centralized state earned Mao and the Party great respect and admiration. Regardless of later misjudgements and errors, Mao enabled China to 'stand up', and that accomplishment alone places him in the category of national hero to many Chinese.

Mao's impact on China also must be assessed in terms of economic and social changes in China after 1949. Despite the setbacks of the Great Leap and the Cultural Revolution, overall China's economy made decided advances during the Maoist period. China's industrial sector grew rapidly and agricultural output was once again showing increases by the time of Mao's death. China's infrastructure expanded with the addition of new railways and improved roads. Electricity became available in all but the most remote villages. Life expectancy reached 65 years by the time of Mao's death, a remarkable increase over the 1949 figure. Under the new laws of the PRC, women held equal status with men and, as a result of the commune movement, worked outside the home. Although efforts to expand education stumbled repeatedly due to political campaigns, the number of literate men and women climbed as schools and colleges grew in number throughout the period. These accomplishments are part of the legacy of the first generation of revolutionary leadership.

At the same time, Maoist policies exacted an enormous human cost. Misguided policy decisions of the Great Leap Forward claimed millions of lives. Whether this cost was levied unintentionally or not, Mao himself chose the policies which led to human disaster and he cannot be absolved of responsibility for the outcomes. When the records of the CCP are someday made available for objective examination, both the Chinese people and the world community will be able to assess more clearly the circumstances that led to the greatest tragedies of the Maoist period and how that experience influenced China's current economic reforms and its political direction.

Despite the disasters that marked the last decade of Mao's life, and the deeply flawed policy decisions made by him and his closest associates, China soon recovered. The resilience of the Chinese people can be clearly seen in the revival of the economy and Chinese society as a whole during the reform era initiated by Deng Xiaoping, as discussed in the next chapter.

CHAPTER FIVE

BUILDING REFORM-ERA CHINA, 1977–89

DENG REVERSES THE MAOIST DIRECTION

From the death of Mao in September 1976 until 1978, maneuvering for power occupied the top government and Party leaders. By 1978, it was clear that Deng Xiaoping and his supporters were the victors in a struggle played out largely behind closed doors. Until his death in 1997, Deng orchestrated a series of reforms that give this era its name.

Major problems faced the new Deng administration: the government now had a 6.5 billion *yuan* deficit; 20 million Chinese were unemployed; and an estimated 100 million were undernourished. The military was woefully out of date, as was China's own technology and scientific research. Thousands of CCP members and wide segments of the population questioned the decisions of the Party leadership. The radical approach of the Maoists, who called for a successor generation of Party faithful more 'Red' than expert, managed to leave China far behind other countries in Asia where the standard of living greatly exceeded that of the average Chinese. If the legacy of the revolutionaries was to mean anything, new approaches to China's many problems were imperative.

Deng and his supporters realized that without economic advances, the future position of the CCP would be untenable. The goal therefore became the succinctly stated 'Four Modernizations' originally put forward by Premier Zhou in the 1970s: modernization of agriculture, industry, national defense, and science and technology. The single most important of the four was the modernization of agriculture because 80% of the population derived their living primarily from agricultural production. Unlike the earlier Maoist policies which were hastily designed and quickly implemented, the new approach called for experimentation with changes in just a few areas before beginning wider reforms. To oversee reform in this vital area of the economy, Deng appointed a close personal supporter, Zhao Ziyang.

Zhao was of a somewhat younger generation of the CCP leadership. Born in 1919, he was only 18 when Japan invaded China in 1937. While still in his teens, he joined the Party and fought in the Second World War.

After the 1949 victory, he rose through the Party ranks in Guangdong province and, after a stint in Inner Mongolia during the Cultural Revolution, was re-assigned to Sichuan, which had suffered tremendously from the violence and chaos of the Cultural Revolution years. In order to speed economic recovery there, in 1975 he began modest reforms which proved very successful. A popular slogan in the province was 'Yao chi liang, zhao Ziyang', meaning, 'If you want food to eat, find Ziyang', the latter phrase being a pun on Zhao's surname which, in the ditty, can be understood as either a surname or the verb 'to find'.

The system used in Sichuan called for renting commune land to individual farming families. The farmers' crops had to be sold to the State at state-mandated prices. Initially land could be leased for only one year, but the early result was so successful that the periods of the lease were extended to three, then five and then 15 years. Also only a percentage of produce had to be sold to the State. The remainder could be sold by the family at newly established 'Free Markets' which sprang up in towns and villages throughout Sichuan. Called the 'contract responsibility system' or responsibility system, the incentives contained within the new system quickly and dramatically increased crop production. Rural incomes doubled. By 1983, 98% of the country's peasant farmers had shifted to the new system. The communes became a part of the past, an economic and social experiment that failed to deliver the pre-1949 promised paradise of the CCP.

Even before the new system was instituted nation-wide, Zhao was given a more important role in Deng's new government. In 1980 he was appointed to the State Council, and as the success of the reforms in Sichuan became apparent, he was named Premier, replacing Hua Guofeng who disappeared into obscurity.

In the 1980s, agricultural production increased an average of 9% a year under the new policies. But equally important to many farm families was the rise of town and township enterprises. By 1989, these small enterprises produced textiles, small electronics or component parts, and plastics; together they accounted for 58% of the total value of rural output. An estimated 25% of them were run by rural women whose financial contribution to family income increased considerably. For the first time in many years, farm families had money to build new houses or new additions to existing homes. The arrival of electricity to even the most remote rural areas allowed the introduction of such luxuries as cassette players, washing machines and televisions. While not every area enjoyed an equal measure of prosperity, the changes in the early 1980s were so dramatic that it was almost like a second revolution. The new slogan was 'To get rich is glorious', and the Chinese embraced the movement with great enthusiasm.

Modernization of industry was more difficult to accomplish. Unlike the farmers, the urban workers had been the primary beneficiaries of the

Maoist period. They enjoyed many benefits which derived from their jobs as workers. An individual was employed by a *danwei* or work unit. In addition to wages, workers had job security, subsidized housing, medical care, pensions and other benefits from their employer, the state. It was virtually impossible to be fired, and lateness, shoddy work or frequent absence were common abuses. Of all urban workers, 96.8% enjoyed such privileges, which could also be passed on to children who were given preference in hiring at their parent's *danwei*.

A majority of government-run enterprises made little or no profit. To change this, in 1984 the government granted autonomy to many state enterprises. Over 400,000 such organizations now could set wages as well as prices; profits could be re-invested to upgrade equipment or to offer workers bonuses. Pressure on unprofitable ventures grew to improve their products and cut losses. Despite the new directives, some ventures continued with business as usual except that complaints and foot-dragging strategies were offered rather than profits. Workers resisted the loss of their 'iron rice bowl' jobs which provided a lifestyle many rural Chinese envied.

But the Deng government was adamant: in the mid-1980s it warned that enterprises which did not make a profit would be closed. To encourage profits, the government lowered the tax on total revenues of an enterprise to only 33%, down from 55% in 1983–84. Still, the progress toward shifting industry to the new system was not smooth. By 1990, 54% of industry remained state-owned and concerns over rising urban unemployment placed further changes on hold.

FOREIGN INVESTMENT AND THE SEZs

As a further stimulus to the economy, in 1980 China secured its first loans from the International Monetary Fund (IMF) and the World Bank. Money became available to upgrade machinery and establish new manufacturing and industrial development. At the same time, another Deng initiative opened China further to Western investment: the Special Economic Zones (SEZs). In 1979, the Deng government opened four southern coastal towns and villages as SEZs: Zhuhai, near Macao; Xiamen, across from Taiwan; Shantou; and Shenzhen, just across the border from Hong Kong. A fifth, Hainan Island, off the southern coast, was added in the 1980s. The advantages of these areas for investors were considerable: the 15% tax was waived for the first and second years of profitability and a 50% tax exemption provided further incentive in the third and fourth years. No import duties were attached to production materials or equipment.

By far the most successful has been Shenzhen, which clearly benefited from its proximity to Hong Kong. The primary foreign investors were Hong Kong and Taiwan Chinese whose investments created a boom town out of a small rural village in a matter of a few years. Attracted by good training and high rates of pay, workers flocked to the town, which boasted the highest annual economic growth rates in all of China by the end of the 1980s. The other SEZs developed more slowly but each boosted local industry to some degree as well as attracting foreign investments. In addition, the government authorized 14 coastal cities to offer special privileges to foreign investors as a further sign of China's new desire to stimulate growth of technology and international trade.

DENG AND THE REORGANIZATION OF THE CCP

Deng himself had been a victim of the extreme Maoist line during the Cultural Revolution. He was aware of the shortcomings of a CCP leadership which had become isolated from the people, just as he was aware of the problems caused throughout China because of poorly educated and inept cadres. Within the Party itself, cadres who had limited education but were considered politically reliable still remained in place at the upper levels of government. At the very highest levels, a small number of elderly men still clung to their positions of power in the Politburo of the CCP's Central Committee. Deng himself was in his eighties, as were several other Party stalwarts.

In 1982, Deng initiated a plan to encourage senior members of the Party to retire. By 1986, a total of 1.8 million had done so. Furthermore, he sought to cleanse the ranks: between 1983 and 1987 the CCP expelled over 150,000 cadres for various forms of wrong-doing (MacFarquhar, 1997: 362). Deng also moved to raise the overall level of education of cadres; as a result of his efforts, 60% of the Party membership below the level of the Politburo soon consisted of younger men and women with college educations. However some elderly members remained at the top of the power structure; Deng appointee Premier Zhao Ziyang, for example, was in his sixties, as was Secretary-General of the CCP Hu Yaobang, another Deng protégé (MacFarquhar, 1997: 336–7).

While the CCP moved to reform itself, Deng remained a committed Communist. He reaffirmed this in proclaiming the Four Cardinal Principles: first, China remained committed to following the socialist road; second, China remained a 'dictatorship of the proletariat' as it continued toward Communism; third, the CCP's leadership was inviolate; and, lastly, Deng proclaimed the supremacy of Marxist–Leninist–Maoist Thought. Any observers who thought they were witnessing the dismantling of China's socialist system needed only to be reminded of the Four Cardinal Principles which, officially at least, maintained the fiction of a government still following the old revolutionary road. Certainly, the CCP maintained its hold over China's society despite the relaxation of economic controls.

This power is illustrated in the discussion (below) of social policies in the 1980s.

FAMILY PLANNING AND THE 'ONE CHILD' POLICY

The government's concern with a burgeoning population in the 1950s initially led to limited campaigns to persuade couples to have fewer children. But it was not until after the Cultural Revolution that greater efforts were made to publicize the need for lowering the country's fertility rate. In the 1970s, the campaign to curtail population growth adopted the slogan 'wan xi shao'. 'Wan', meaning late, asked couples to delay marriage and child bearing; 'xi shao', meaning fewer, referred to waiting longer between children and bearing fewer children overall. As part of this campaign, peasant families were asked to limit families to three children; by 1977 the number dropped to two. This phase of the campaign was successful, lowering fertility rates from six to three children per woman (Greenhalgh, 1994).

In 1980, a new version of the 1950 Marriage Law was announced, requiring all married couples to use a form of birth control. The law did not specifically call for a 'one-child' limit, but local regulations and national publicity campaigns made it clear that one child per family was the goal of the new campaign. The actual implementation of the law varied from province to province, and each area could establish rewards for compliance as well as penalties for ignoring the new regulations. The five autonomous regions' minority populations were initially exempted from the new one child limit, but by 1986 these areas, too, were urged to institute one-child limits in urban areas and two-children limits in rural districts.

The pressure on urban populations all over China was great. Penalties could be harsh, including fines of up to 15% of a family's annual income and no free schooling or health care for an unauthorized second child. There were abuses of power as local family planning officials struggled to adhere to quotas imposed by higher authorities: forced late-term abortions and abandoned baby girls were part of the price of the new policy in some instances. Most family planning authorities preferred women to use an IUD (intrauterine device) which, from their viewpoint, was cheaper and more reliable than other forms of contraception as well as having the advantage of giving control of a woman's fertility to the doctor who inserted and removed the IUD. Only with permission could a doctor remove an IUD and allow a second pregnancy.

Undermining the national efforts to control population, however, was the new economic system. As China reverted to family farms, the family once again became the basic economic unit in the countryside. The more sons in a family, the more hands to work the land and the more income the family would share. In the 1980s, girls still 'married out', following the traditional exogamy of village China; a family with only a single daughter would lose that pair of hands upon the girl's marriage, while a son would not only remain at home, but would also bring in another worker, his wife, to increase the family's fortune. By reinforcing the patriarchal values of China, the family planning policy undermined earlier efforts to improve the status of women and to break away from old patterns of male dominance (Jacka, 1997).

Some groups found ways around the rules. The 'floating population' was not monitored by family planning officials because it was transient; children born to women who joined this migratory group were thus outside the plan. But even peasant families found ways around the regulations, and the policy clearly did not have 100% compliance. Nonetheless, China's official rate of population growth fell to 1.1, one of the lowest in the world. In 1988, many rural areas modified their policies so that rural families whose first child was female usually received permission to have a second child.

THE 'OPENING' OF CHINESE SOCIETY IN THE 1980s

During the 1980s, China's new openness allowed many Chinese their first glimpses of the wider world beyond China's border. Access to translations of Western literature and the arrival of Hollywood films in towns across China boosted the demand for publications and entertainments of all kinds. Chinese authors and film producers found new audiences for their work as government regulation at last relaxed. One popular new genre was the 'scar' literature that detailed the misery which had afflicted so many during the period of the Cultural Revolution. One shared theme in much of this writing was the devastating impact of the movement on individual lives. These accounts made clear the authors' views that they had been manipulated into joining a movement which cost some of them their families, their chance for a good education and their self-respect. A growing number of these works found their way into English as the 'ten lost years' of 1966–76 became a part of history (Gao, 1987; Liang and Shapiro, 1983; Ma, 1996; Yue, 1985) [*Docs 11 and 12*].

As workers and peasants at last prospered, new styles of clothing in brighter colors emerged on China's streets. Privately-owned restaurants offered appetizing food and snacks, and road-side vendors sold fruits and vegetables grown in local gardens. Music tapes of Hong Kong and Taiwan singers circulated through the country, along with China's own rising generation of rock musicians. Discos opened in many cities, although the official hours usually required such establishments to close relatively early. Dancers and practitioners of traditional exercises, like the slow movements of *Taijiquan* (T'ai Ch'i) and *qigong*, gathered in public parks in the early morning hours to enjoy decidedly apolitical activities. Although these new pleasures were small, everyday matters, the chance to enjoy daily life was, in itself, a sign of renewal.

But the more open atmosphere also meant less oversight of officials at all levels in the vast Chinese bureaucracy. Some officials found opportunities to enrich themselves and their friends in the changed atmosphere. Among the crimes officially reported and denounced in the press during the 1980s were embezzling state property, smuggling Western-made products, and taking bribes. Periodically, police crack-downs resulted in large numbers of arrests; those convicted often received stiff penalties, from years in prison to death. Nonetheless, large and small-scale corruption continued as China's economy expanded at an ever-faster pace.

Long-suppressed crimes like prostitution and drug trafficking also re-emerged, along with the economic reforms. The punishments for both of these crimes could be as extreme as the death penalty, but as profits from these activities grew, the number of people willing to take the risks involved also increased. Sales of pornography and increasing incidences of sexually transmitted diseases reinforced conservatives' claims that China had gone too far in opening its doors to the decadent West.

CHANGES IN MINORITY REGIONS

China also witnessed a new restlessness among its minority populations in the 1980s. Although the policy of regional autonomy was considered China's solution to 'the nationalities question', the policies of the Maoist period had confirmed for some minorities their belief that the Han Chinese did not respect or value minorities or minority culture. Minorities welcomed the reforms of the 1980s, as did other Chinese citizens, but their welcome quickly changed to dismay as the Central Government announced new plans to develop the rich natural resources of some of the autonomous regions. Beijing also appeared to encourage Han Chinese to move to the border regions, and as word spread of readily available land and other incentives, the numbers of Chinese heading west increased. In response, students in minorities areas organized demonstrations in major towns and cities. Just as Han Chinese students in China proper demonstrated for change, so did minority students who also hoped for true autonomy in addition to greater democracy and economic freedom.

Of particular concern to the government were activities in oil-rich Xinjiang, home to the Uighurs, a Muslim group numbering some 8 million people in the 1980s. Xinjiang was the site of secessionist governments in 1933 and 1944, both of which sought to overthrow Chinese-dominated provincial governments and establish an independent East Turkestan

Republic. The last of these still controlled three of the region's districts in 1949 when the PLA marched into the area and struck an agreement with the Nationalist officials still holding on to power there. In an effort to gain support of the Uighurs and other Muslim groups in Xinjiang, the PRC promised cultural autonomy and assistance with economic development. Instead, it sent hundreds of poor Chinese who were relocated to the region by the government in the late 1950s. Many of these new settlers scratched out a living on land reclaimed from the deserts, while others worked in the region's oil fields or coal mines. The Cultural Revolution brought more Han to the region, along with fighting, desecration of Muslim mosques, burning of the Qur'an, and prison sentences for outspoken Uighurs and other minorities. Although the military restored order in Xinjiang in 1969, the aftermath of the violent phase of the Cultural Revolution continued with the suppression of religious activities through to 1976. It was not surprising, therefore, that even after Uighurs and other Muslims were finally allowed to worship publicly once more, relations between the Chinese population and the Muslims remained strained.

When the Reform Era began, Xinjiang's Muslims sought to make their voices heard. Demonstrations became a part of urban life in the major cities; even the regional capital, Urumqi, which was a Han Chinese stronghold, saw student demonstrations in the 1980s. Some of the students' complaints mirrored those elsewhere in China: corruption, inflation, and abuses of power. Other complaints were more specifically related to the region's minority status: Uighurs opposed the population control policy; they wanted an end to Han migration which had increased Han presence from 5% to 40% of the population; and they demanded that nuclear testing in the Lop Nor area of the Takla Makan desert stop. The government condemned the demonstrations and increased vigilance and arrests, rather than acknowledging the legitimacy of these requests.

Other minorities fared better in the reform era. For example, Muslim Chinese, or Hui as they are officially called in China, reacted vigorously when books deemed insulting to Islam appeared on bookstore shelves in their autonomous area, Ningxia. In that instance, the offending book was pulled from bookstore shelves and the Muslim leaders were mollified with apologies. Privileging one minority group over another, however, was viewed in some quarters as a 'divide and rule' tactic which meant that each group struggled alone for privileges or concessions from the government. With the CCP ultimately determining policy in minority areas, the prospects for true autonomy over local cultural affairs still seemed as remote as ever.

THE DEMOCRACY MOVEMENT AND TIANANMEN SQUARE

As the reform era continued to breathe new life into China's economy, many observers of these dramatic changes could be forgiven for thinking that the economic liberalization of the government would inevitably have to extend to greater personal freedom and a more democractic and open political system. Certainly, students and intellectuals across China equated economic reform with political reform. The younger generation especially welcomed the changes initiated by Deng.

Their increased expectations quickly turned to public calls for greater changes, in particular democratization. Even as the first reforms were being announced in 1978, students began posting *Dazibao* or Big Character Posters on university campuses calling for rapid advances toward political liberalization. In the fall of 1978, the southern walls of the Forbidden City on Changan Boulevard in the center of Beijing carried student and worker posters calling for more freedoms and faster change. Dubbed 'Democracy Wall', the area became a meeting place for students and urban residents of all walks of life who gathered at the wall to listen to speeches and voice their own complaints about the existing system. In December of 1978, posters criticizing Deng himself began to appear, but despite this new provocation, no action was taken to curtail the movement. With the inauguration of what became known as the Democracy Movement in 1978, it appeared that a new era had, indeed, begun.

One of the more outspoken leaders was Wei Jingsheng, a young worker who called on the Deng government to institute a 'Fifth Modernization', democracy. Wei's call was taken up by students who continued to flock to the wall in early 1979. Abruptly, on 29 March 1979, the government arrested Wei and accused him of crimes against the state. A one-day show trial in October 1979 ended with Wei receiving a 15-year sentence, most of it to be spent in solitary confinement. In December, 'Democracy Wall' was moved to a more remote and inaccessible part of Beijing. The next year, the 'Four Big Rights', dating from the Cultural Revolution period and included in the 1978 Constitution, were revoked: citizens no longer had the rights of *daming*, *dafang*, *dabianlun*, and *dazibao*, or, the rights to speak out freely, air views fully, hold great debates and write Big Character posters. At the same time, the government began quiet investigation and detention of the most active supporters of the Democracy Movement. An estimated 100,000 people were arrested and sent for re-education in rural areas. Those from outside the major cities had their residence permits revoked, a measure intended to limit further the concentration of pro-democracy advocates in urban areas.

These efforts to quiet, or at least tone down, critics inside China did not work. Increasingly disenchanted with the pace of the reforms and the refusal of the government to allow greater personal and political freedom, outspoken individuals continued to challenge the government. Among them was the highly regarded physicist Fang Lizhi, a popular professor at the China University of Science and Technology (CUST), in Hefei, Anhui province. The Russian-educated Fang had once worked on a top-secret government project, a heavy-water nuclear reactor. But in 1957 he was expelled from the Party for criticizing the politicization of the physics curriculum: his physics text quoted Lenin who, for political reasons, rejected the theories of renown physicist Niels Bohr. Nonetheless, China's great need for educated individuals meant that Fang was eventually allowed to work at CUST. During the Cultural Revolution, however, he was labeled a 'stinking intellectual' and was relegated to the countryside where he labored in rice fields and helped dig a railway tunnel. After the death of Mao, he was reinstated and even allowed to go abroad to attend scientific conferences. His stature as a scientist led to his appointment as Vice President of CUST where he enjoyed the support of many of his colleagues and students in the 1980s. In 1985, a student demonstration at his university drew over 17,000 people who called for greater reform. The following year, Fang gave a speech in which he said that the socialist movement was a failure and that China needed not only modernization but also Westernization if the country was to advance (Fang, 1991). This time, he was relieved of his duties at CUST and, in 1987, was appointed to a research institute in Beijing where he could be watched more closely. Despite the government monitoring, he continued to speak out, calling for more reforms [*Doc. 13*].

Fang was not alone in his outspoken comments. Others also criticized the system and suffered accordingly. For example, Liu Binyan, a journalist, investigated stories of official corruption and, for his efforts, was expelled from the CCP. He left for the United States where he became an active member of human rights organizations.

Despite the dangers involved and the possibility of severe repercussions from the authorities, intellectuals continued to speak their minds. In an effort to dampen student interest in hearing such views, in 1986 the government announced new regulations for all college graduates that required two years of assigned labor before they began their chosen careers. Worse, from a student perspective, was that 30% of each graduating class had to accept jobs assigned by the government. Students saw this for what it was: a means by which to curtail criticism from China's best educated people. Angered by the new rules and disgruntled over low stipends (virtually all university students at that time were supported by monthly government payments) and poor living conditions, student dissatisfaction simmered.

Disagreements emerged within the higher echelons of the Party. Hu Yaobang, Deng's hand-picked leader of the CCP, made no secret of his opposition to the new rules. As a result, Hu was dismissed from his post in

1987. China's students immediately embraced him as a hero for championing their cause.

In 1988, student organizers decided to circulate a petition calling for greater reforms. Stirred by the daring speeches and writings of men like Fang Lizhi and their own student leaders, their list of demands began with a call for modernizaton and democracy. The summer of 1988 saw demonstrations in cities across China; during the academic year of 1988–89 campus unrest continued.

The catalyst for the massive demonstrations that led to the dramatic and tragic events in Beijing on 4 June 1989, was the unexpected death of Hu Yaobang on 15 April 1989, from a heart attack. His loss galvanized students, who organized a mass memorial service in Tiananmen Square, at the very center of the nation's capital. But what began as a memorial for Hu quickly grew into mass demonstrations. Day after day that April, students, workers, and ordinary Beijing residents paraded to the square, calling on the government to institute greater democracy and end the growing corruption among officials. Some marchers carried signs to air grievances or to criticize specific government policies.

Although the government repeatedly ordered the marchers to disperse and to leave the square, students and their supporters continued to gather there. On 26 April 1989, the government denounced the students in an editorial in China's official newspaper, the *People's Daily*. The still-peaceful demonstrators were called 'conspirators' and their actions were labeled illegal. By officially denouncing the students and their allies, the government raised the stakes. Students now feared reprisals. To protect themselves by legitimizing their demonstrations, students not only continued to rally in Tiananmen Square, but also demanded a dialogue with top government leaders to present their views. On 27 April, over 50,000 students and their supporters crowded the streets of the capital, cheered by residents. The movement was dubbed 'Beijing Spring' and appeared to augur a new age of democracy for China.

Many among this generation of students saw themselves as heirs to the May Fourth Movement of 1919. In honor of that earlier generation, which had also sacrificed so much in order to save its country 70 years earlier, the students held yet another major demonstration on 4 May 1989. Police efforts to control the massive demonstration were ineffectual, and students flooded into the center of the national capital once more.

The CCP clearly faced a difficult predicament. To complicate matters further, in the middle of May, Mikhail Gorbachev, the architect of Soviet reforms and *perestroika*, was scheduled to arrive in Beijing, the first visit to China by a Russian leader since 1959. This historic visit would be covered by the international news media, representatives of which had begun to arrive in Beijing. The occupation of the city center by thousands of students was becoming more than a national embarrassment for the CCP: it now would be televised for an international audience. Unrelenting, the students decided to call a hunger strike and in doing so galvanized even greater popular support and sympathy. Ultimately, the Gorbachev visit took place as scheduled but the usual welcome ceremonies in Tiananmen Square had to be abandoned. To the great embarrassment of the leadership, students held up signs calling for *perestroika* and Russian-style *glasnost* as foreign media filmed the student-jammed square.

It is important to note that Beijing was not the only city to experience what came to be called 'Beijing Spring'. Students in other major cities followed the example of their friends in Beijing and launched their own demonstrations. Some students made the long and expensive journey to Beijing to record the impassioned speeches, interspersed with rock music by some of China's biggest rock stars, and then returned home to play the recordings over loud-speaker systems at their home universities. Thousands of students all across China were joined by workers in mass demonstrations calling for greater government reform, and cities like Shanghai, Wuhan, Guangzhou, and Xian witnessed an outpouring of criticism mixed with the exuberance of popular music.

On 18 May, the stand-off in Beijing took a new turn. The Prime Minister, Li Peng, agreed to a televised interview with students leaders, including some still on a hunger strike. Wang Dan and Wuerkaixi were among the student representatives chosen to meet the top leaders of the CCP. The exchange between the youthful leadership and the top men of the CCP included repeated student demands for the government to listen to the people and to enter into a dialogue with them about China's future. The stoney face of Prime Minister Li, filmed at the end of the interview, suggested that the patience of the Party leadership had come to an end.

What must have been an angry and frustrated Central Committee finally voted on 20 May to impose martial law. Only Zhao Ziyang, Deng's appointed heir-apparent, opposed this move. As a result, he lost his standing in the CCP and was dismissed from his post as Secretary-General on 24 May. He was subsequently placed under house arrest. As for the students, they simply ignored the announcement and continued their occupation of Tiananmen Square.

To boost morale and keep the number of demonstrators high, celebrity rock stars visited the square. They also provided a welcome diversion for the hundreds of students with impromptu rock concerts which served to draw even more onlookers and participants to the center of the city. Art students from Beijing contributed a statue they called the Goddess of Liberty, which they erected just opposite the painting of Chairman Mao over the central gate at the north end of the square. The atmosphere combined the tension of a political movement with the spirit of a rock concert.

At the end of May, students still occupied the square, but word spread that troops were arriving in the capital. The situation became extremely tense. Student leaders called for a vote on whether or not they should remain in Tiananmen Square, where hunger-striking students had drawn new supporters to their cause. Although at one point a majority voted to end the demonstration, a minority of student leaders were joined by newly-arrived students who wanted the movement to continue. So, despite the efforts of professors sympathetic to the students to persuade them to end their occupation, hundreds of students chose to remain.

On 3 June, troops brought to the Beijing area from outlying regions began to converge on the center of the city. On 4 June 1989, in the early hours of the morning, armed units advanced on the square itself, shooting at random to disperse on-lookers who threw stones or shouted epithets. Gun-fire thus preceded the military push to clear demonstrators from Tiananmen Square once and for all. Shocked Beijingers rushed bloodied victims to local hospitals, and as the troops advanced, the toll of dead and wounded rose. Last-minute negotiations between the students and the military allowed the final band of demonstrators gathered at the south end of the square to leave. As they marched away, leaving behind the debris of weeks of occupation, they sang the international anthem of Communism, the 'Internationale'.

In the chaos of 3 and 4 June, the number of dead was impossible to ascertain. Later estimates varied from the hundreds to the thousands, and even a decade later the final number of fatalities was still disputed. But the grisly photographs of that night and the day after show bodies still caught in wreckage around the city of Beijing as well as bodies piled in some Beijing hospital corridors. The military secured the square and cleaned up the mess in the days that followed. The official press in China denounced the entire movement as 'counter-revolutionary' and castigated its leadership [*Doc. 14*]. The government-controlled media publicized the arrest warrants issued for students leaders and outspoken critics like Fang Lizhi, who sought refuge in the US embassy with his family. He remained there for a year before being allowed to leave China. Student leaders fled underground, and a number of them eventually made their way abroad. The latter included Wang Dan and Wuerkaixi, a young Uighur whose name is more accurately romanized as Erkesh Devlet. Both had been among the student representatives to interview Li Peng on television just weeks earlier. The most prominent woman leader, Chai Ling, also escaped, eventually making her way to the United States. Less fortunate students were caught in the crackdown which followed in the summer of 1989. Some of China's most promising young students soon began prison sentences; while the most outspoken sat in solitary confinement, others were sent for *laogai* or 'reform through labor' in the often harsh conditions of labor camps.

The international aftermath included broken cultural exchanges and a temporary halt to foreign investment. The most pessimistic observers felt that in one horrific night the CCP had lost all that it had gained in the preceding decade. Certainly the hoped-for democratization of China was seen as an ever more distant dream, as the optimistic 1980s ended in Beijing's Tiananmen Square.

CHAPTER SIX

DEEPENING REFORM: CHINA IN THE 1990s

Following the Beijing Spring of 1989, the CCP teetered on the edge of another dramatic policy shift, away from the economic reforms which had improved the lives of so many. Conservatives in the Party reasserted their position, warning once more of the dangers of change and using the example of urban disorder in support of their claims.

However, instead of a reversal, other events in the communist world shifted the balance toward a continuation of the reforms and the 'opening up' of China to the outside. In 1991, the USSR collapsed under the weight of growing internal political issues and a shattered economy. The constituent republics of the former communist giant found themselves independent for the first time in 70 years, and Russia itself began a new life as a republic. China's former mentor and economic model was gone, and its failings were exposed for all to see.

In response to these dramatic international events, Deng moved quickly to reinvigorate the reforms of the 1980s. His highly publicized visit to the dynamic southern province of Guangdong in 1992 signaled that China would press on with its new direction, away from a centrally planned economy and toward an increasingly market-driven system. Although Deng was 88 years old that year and no longer active in the day-to-day affairs of the Party, his decision to move forward with China's reforms ensured the continuing expansion of the Chinese economy.

At the head of the government was the newly appointed Jiang Zemin. Born in 1926, Jiang represented what is referred to in China as the 'third generation' of CCP leadership. Jiang joined the CCP during the Second World War and served in the military. After 1949, he was among the young Chinese sent for education in the USSR where he learned Russian and received a degree in engineering. After a stint working in an auto plant, he held a series of Central Government posts, and by 1985 his experience earned him the position of mayor of Shanghai, where he also held the top Party post. His technical training helped to launch Shanghai's renewal: the city had languished for years with little government support to the former stronghold of colonialism and imperialism. Under Jiang, Shanghai began its rennaisaance, paving the way for its key role in international trade and foreign investment in the 1990s. In 1987, he was named to the CCP's Politburo. During the student-led demonstrations of 1989, Jiang managed to defuse the situation in Shanghai, which could have been the site of a Tiananmen-style crackdown without Jiang's cautious reponse. This success doubtless contributed to Deng's decision to bring Jiang to Beijing to replace the disgraced Zhao Ziyang in June 1989. As a transitional figure between the old guard and the new, Jiang was well prepared to continue Deng's efforts to accelerate modernization and economic reform.

Also at the top of the Party hierarchy in the 1990s was Prime Minister Li Peng. Born in 1928, Li's father was executed by the Nationalists for his leftist sympathies in 1930. Li became the adopted child of Zhou Enlai and his wife, Deng Yingzhao, who raised a number of children whose parents died in the political and military struggle prior to 1949. Like Jiang, Li was also educated in the USSR, returning to China in 1955 with a degree in engineering. With Zhou's support, he rose through the Party ranks and by the 1980s was serving as one of five vice premiers under Zhao Ziyang. When Zhao was moved to the post of Secretary-General of the CCP in 1987, Li was promoted to Acting Premier and then Premier of China. After 1989, Li was widely blamed for the shootings at Tiananmen Square and rumors that he was to be removed continued throughout the 1990s.

Behind both men, however, was Deng himself, who continued to counter the complaints and protests of the ageing coterie of conservatives whose numbers continued to dwindle as the decade progressed. In 1997, weakened by illnesses associated with advanced old age, Deng himself passed away at the age of 93. Although some observers in and outside of China had surmised that President Jiang would falter without his powerful backer, such was not the case. Jiang consolidated his position in the Party and with the military to remain firmly at the top of the power structure. His guidance continued to move China along the path of economic reform and away from the destructive policies of the Maoist years.

ECONOMIC GROWTH IN THE 1990s

By 1995, headway had been made in dismantling the inefficient and unprofitable government-run enterprises. Approximately 34% of businesses and industries were run by the state; another 37% were classified as collective ownership, which referred to an array of ownership forms ranging from small village or township businesses to workshops run by the workers or local governments; 29% were classified as privately owned and operated. In 1996, China's State Statistical Bureau reported that more than one in 12 workers were employed by private (*siying*) enterprises, and that over

25 million individual businesses and 650,000 privately run enterprises produced 14.6% of China's GDP (Parris, 1999: 267) [*Doc. 15*]. China's state-run enterprises, which continued to employ two-thirds of China's urban work force, contributed less than half of China's economic output. The private sector was clearly the most dynamic part of the economy and it was the source of wealth for China's first multi-millionaires: 2–5% of all the private enterprise owners had incomes over 10 million *yuan* by the middle of the 1990s (Parris, 1999: 267).

This new system of public and private ownership was referred to as 'socialism with Chinese characteristics', in China, but outside the country another term was coined to describe the hybrid system – 'authoritarian capitalism'. Both terms have come to describe a system that is partly under close government control, particularly in banking and internal trade of commodities, but also partly free to expand and develop new products and new markets. China became a land of joint-ventures, enterprises with foreign funding and/or investors but with Chinese public agencies as partners. In addition, the SEZs (introduced in Chapter 5) continued to draw new foreign investment to China and to provide training for hundreds of Chinese workers.

During the 1990s, the number of agricultural workers steadily declined as more and more opportunities were created by the burgeoning economy. From a high of some 70% employed in agriculture or related work at the beginning of the reform era, the numbers steadily declined to less than 50% by the middle of the 1990s (Goldman and MacFarquhar, 1999: 41). With better paid options in the towns and cities available, and more mobility for the working population tolerated by the government, the urban population also grew during the 1990s. As a result, parts of rural China experienced a marked 'feminization of agriculture' as young men sought seasonal or even permanent work in the cities, leaving their wives and children to manage the family's leased farm land.

Young women seeking an escape from what could be harsh conditions in rural areas also sought work in the city. Usually they ended up in low-paying factory jobs but, from their viewpoint, these were still desirable as their salaries allowed them to enjoy some of the pleasures of city life as well as to send money to their parents back home. Factories in Shenzhen, for example, took advantage of this labor pool by hiring the young women on short-term contracts which did not require the company to provide the benefits that went with hiring long-term employees. Any worker who proved difficult could be easily fired and replaced from the readily available pool of rural women hoping for a period of adventure before marrying and settling down (Lee, 1998).

INCREASING DISPARITY BETWEEN URBAN AND RURAL CHINA

The greatest economic prosperity of the 1990s occurred in the urban areas and, in particular, along China's coast. As these cities courted foreign investment and encouraged new housing, roads, and transport systems, the look of China's urban environment changed dramatically. In the 1990s, some cities called themselves 'City of Cranes' because of the great number of building cranes that crowded China's urban skies. The pounding of pile drivers reverberated through downtown Shanghai and Beijing as new high-rise buildings rose from what had been neighborhoods of old-style tile-roof houses. Privately-owned apartments offered all modern amenities to their new owners, who also frequented the new night clubs and restaurants in places like Nanjing and Guangzhou. Cell phones (called *Dageda* or Big Brother in Chinese) and pagers became *de rigeur* for the up-and-coming young businessman. Those who had succeeded in the new economy also bought personal computers, and by the end of the decade, over 17 million Chinese subscribed to an Internet service. For a new generation of young educated Chinese, the 1990s clearly offered the kind of life inconceivable to those of their parents' generation.

While urban incomes rose, however, rural incomes changed more slowly. On average, city-dwellers enjoyed double the income of their rural counterparts in the 1990s. Unlike urban and coastal China, the hinterland still had areas without an adequate electricity supply, elementary schools or health care. Conditions in the poorest areas remained difficult, and the possibility of a comfortable lifestyle still seemed an unobtainable goal.

Adding to the woes of some poorer areas, farm families without good connections found themselves the target of increasing exactions from local officials. Although the terms of a farm lease called for set amounts in taxes and rent, local officials increasingly added levies of various kinds. Some of these funds were ostensibly to be used for local roads or irrigation projects, but other taxes or fees, simply labeled miscellaneous or occasional taxes, made people both angry and suspicious. They believed that the money they worked so hard for was disappearing into the pockets of lazy and corrupt officials. Peasant-farmers resented these additional payments, but many found themselves unable to avoid the added financial demands. As in previous periods of change in China, those at the bottom once more found themselves at the mercy of local officials. Complaints against these exactions led some angry farmers to demonstrate in town centers and to denounce local officials publicly. The usual response from the government was to arrest the farmers who were considered to be the ringleaders of the demonstration and to allow local officials to remain in their posts. Without local accountability of officials, the levies appeared likely to continue.

It was therefore of great interest to observers both in and outside China when the CCP moved to allow a more open elective process to develop at the local level. Moves in this direction began with the Organic Law of Villagers' Committees, which came into effect in 1988. The law was intended to allow villagers a greater say in the management of their village and greater autonomy for elected village officers. According to the law, all adult residents of the villages had a right to vote and stand for election to a three-year term on their village committees, which varied in size from three to seven members. Although the 1989 demonstrations in Beijing threatened to de-rail this reform, in the 1990s many villages did, indeed, hold elections in which they chose their local officials from among competing candidates. In 1997, the CCP leadership reaffirmed its commitment to the Organic Law which, for the first time since 1949, gave rural residents the power to rid themselves of the most incompetent or corrupt village officials. Although corruption (discussed below) continued to influence village elections at the end of the 1990s, the new rules offered the prospect of greater accountability among officials at the lowest level.

CHINA AFTER DENG XIAOPING

After Deng's death in 1997, President Jiang moved out from under his predecessor's shadow. Although domestic matters took precedence, President Jiang took on an increasingly visible role in international relations. His understanding of international affairs was arguably stronger than that of all earlier leaders, including Deng Xiaoping, and Jiang seemed relatively more comfortable on foreign visits. His ability to speak English even enabled him to give the occasional interview to visiting English-speaking journalists. In the 1990s, both his sons went to the United States to study and returned with American graduate degrees. Jiang himself visited the United States in 1997, and despite clear differences with the American leadership over issues such as human rights, the visit heightened his status at home.

After 1997, Jiang's position was further strengthened when Li Peng followed constitutional law and stepped down as Prime Minister. Li was still widely blamed for the shootings at Tiananmen Square in 1989, and some observers saw this as a positive development for Jiang's presidency. Li did not disappear, however: he became Chairman of the National People's Congress for 1999–2000, and remained popular among Party conservatives. However, his position was weakened in 2000 when his protégé, Cheng Kejie, Vice Chairman of the NPC, was executed for corruption.

Jiang replaced Li with a valued colleague from his Shanghai days, the dynamic and reform-minded Zhu Rongji. Zhu was promoted to Executive Deputy Prime Minister in 1993 and to Prime Minister in 1998. Additional Jiang supporters in key government positions included a woman, Chen Zhili, who became Minister of Education, and Zeng Peiyan, Minister of

State Development and Planning Commission, and close adviser Zeng Qinghong, who became head of the CCP's Organization Department in 1999 (Gilley, 1999: 249–50).

Like all Chinese leaders, Jiang's position at the head of the Party and the civilian government also made him the commanding officer of all branches of the military. To ensure continuing military support for his presidency, he provided additional funding for much needed modernization of all branches of the military establishment.

Jiang's administration also remained dedicated to Deng-style reforms. To continue forward momentum, Jiang reaffirmed the need for China to upgrade its production methods and management techniques. China's economy continued to grow, although the Asian economic crisis of 1997–98 slightly slowed the percentage of growth. Nonetheless, China made remarkable strides in expanding its economy, and by the end of the decade, China enjoyed the world's third largest GDP, measured in purchasing power parity (Meisner, 1999: 245).

POPULAR CULTURE IN THE 1990s

As China continued its opening process and the reforms of the 1990s deepened, new forms of entertainment and pastimes emerged. From the young post-Mao generation to the retired workers who had seen such dramatic changes in their lifetimes, people participated in voluntary spare-time activities that brought pleasure rather than political indoctrination.

One strong indicator of the degree of change was the emergence of new forms of literature. The 'scar' accounts of the 1980s gave way to the 1990s 'beautiful writers', young women who wrote of their careers and, in a bold departure from earlier writings, of their love life. The new atmosphere in China fostered a more outspoken and adventurous urban woman, who attracted young reading audiences despite the fact that the books themselves were often quickly banned by the authorities. The resulting caché seemed to add to, rather than detract from, their followings.

Young people were increasingly drawn to discos and clubs in towns and cities all over the country. Western-style rock music, by both Western and Chinese groups, made buildings vibrate late at night. More sedate but no less popular were the dancing clubs organized by older citizens: in the early evenings, groups of retired folks performed traditional dances to the accompaniment of drums, enjoying themselves on warm summer nights. Other new sounds in China included karaoke clubs, which, as elsewhere in Asia, subjected audiences to fractured versions of classic and modern music from the East and the West.

Some newly available forms of entertainment were of a more educational nature. Urban families enrolled their single offspring in innumerable after-school activities like piano, dance or martial arts lessons as parents sought to give their child the opportunities and pleasures they themselves never had. Although rural children continued to work on the family farm after school, the aspirations of parents with smaller numbers of children also rose in village China where the modest pleasures of a generally better diet and wider access to radio and television brought color to the lives of millions.

Sports, always popular in China, drew new recruits. The possibility of joining a professional or semi-professional sport team encouraged young men to hone their skills. Sports leagues formed to compete with neighboring towns or provinces, and posters of sports stars were included in many of the new magazines available on street corners all over the country. Thousands of people simply enjoyed the opportunity for a game of table tennis, billiards, or various forms of chess.

In many ways, the decade of the 1990s was a pivotal one for Chinese society. Although it had begun with many people still in shock over the 1989 shootings in Tiananmen Square, it ended with greater prosperity, for larger numbers of people, than in any other decade of the twentieth century. Ironically, that dramatic change was possible only because of the rejection of Mao's vision of creating a socialist society in just one generation.

CHAPTER SEVEN

NEW SOCIETY, NEW CHALLENGES

Many of the changes in China after the death of Mao in 1976 received broad popular support from the majority of the Chinese people and, in general, the 1980s and 1990s were decades of hope. Prosperity reached into the countryside as farmers set their own prices for their products and built new homes or added new rooms to the old ones. More opportunities for education, and even for travel within China, opened new doors for many, who saw the new government policies as the answer to China's – and their own – future prosperity.

Yet the changes gave rise to unanticipated problems and new challenges for the CCP. While some of the problems may become less acute as China's economic growth is better distributed across all segments of the population, others will require concerted effort if they are to be resolved. Surveyed below are some of the areas of development that have emerged as issues for Chinese society as a whole and for the CCP in particular. These include China's growing pollution and its negative impact on the environment and human health; the continuing increase in crime, corruption and vices such as prostitution and trafficking in women; growing discontent over limits on religious practice; and the need for greater equity in access to education and employment. Despite these difficulties, as the final section in this chapter shows, there is great pride in today's China, and the emergence of a new nationalism among the younger generation may prove strong enough to buoy China as it confronts the various issues outlined below.

POLLUTION AND THE ENVIRONMENT

China's environmental record is not atypical of nation-states undergoing rapid modernization. In the 1950s, the Great Leap Forward contributed to the process of environmental degradation through over-hasty policy decisions which did not take into account their impact on the environment. Cutting of trees and brush to fuel the backyard steel furnaces sped deforestation all over China and compounded the annual flooding as denuded ground shed water. In the north and northwest, there was an increase in desertification as China's major deserts threatened to cover precious arable land. The use of coal to fuel and heat homes meant that pollution continued to harm air quality; as the urban population grew in the reform period, the increased emissions intensified the pollution levels, as did an increase in the number of vehicles, none of which were required to have pollution-reducing catalytic converters.

The increase in small and middle-sized enterprises in the late 1970s and throughout the reform period placed further stress on waterways which were already polluted by industrial waste from state-run enterprises. Farm land run-off included 'night soil' (untreated human feces) which was still used as the most common fertilizer in rural China. Added to this was a mix of fertilizer and insecticide chemicals that entered rivers and streams as farmers attempted to force crops from marginal land.

The growing problem obviously needed attention, and in 1998 the government created the State Environment Protection Administration to address poor air and water quality. The new agency was empowered to enforce existing laws, and in a number of cases it imposed fines on polluters. Unfortunately, the payment of the fine did not always end the polluting practice.

China also attempted to provide protection to some of the country's endangered animal species. A national and international campaign raised money to preserve the panda's natural habitat, but as of 2000 the endangered black and white herbivore was still safer in a zoo than in the wild. The same was true for northeastern China's Siberian tiger. In central China, the Yangzi river dolphin remained in difficulty despite efforts to protect it from fishermen. As ecotourism gains in popularity in China and elsewhere, China may find greater incentives to preserve the most rare aspects of its natural heritage.

China's efforts to raise the standard of living has, invariably, raised concerns when major projects appear to threaten the existing environment. One of the most controversial issues of the 1990s, both in and outside China, has been the Three Gorges Dam, which, when completed, will be the world's largest hydroelectric project. At a cost of US$24.5 billion it will also be the world's most expensive. Among the varied impacts of the new dam are the relocation of 1.2 million people, whose homes and farmland will be inundated, and the loss of important archaeological sites. Conservationists and critics warn that the dam's location over a seismically active area is a time bomb. Further, the Yangzi River, the world's third-largest, carries a great deal of sediment which could threaten the actual workings of the dam; because much of the upstream water contains untreated human waste, the build-up of pollutants may prove yet another disastrous consequence. On the other hand, if the project works as planned, it will supply one-tenth of all China's electrical power, may help control flooding all along the river, and will allow a great increase in the amount of shipping tonnage throughout the Yangzi River valley, a distance of over 1,000 miles. Only after the dam's completion, marked for 2009, will these questions be answered.

CRIME, CORRUPTION AND VICE

Overall, the crime rate in China compared to that of developed countries remained low during the 1990s. As noted in a recent study, China also has had a smaller number of people in prison relative to the size of its population than in the West: the United States, for example, imprisons people at double the Chinese rate (Seymour, 1999). On the other hand, Chinese law allows much harsher penalties: its law code calls for execution as punishment for over 200 crimes. The judicial system has been accused of tolerating the use of brute force in dealing with prisoners and also for a lack of due process. For example, in the 'Strike Hard' campaign, which began in the middle of the 1990s, police increased the rate of arrests across China, detaining thousands of men and women whose crimes ranged from petty theft to arson and murder. The campaign was clearly a warning to criminals that it would be a mistake to interpret the new economic freedoms as an invitation to engage in illegal activities. Although the campaign had its internal critics, in general many Chinese supported it, as well as the harsh treatment meted out to criminals. The persuasive rationale has been that strong punishment is necessary if China is to enjoy relative stability.

Despite the efforts of the 'Strike Hard' campaign and continuing vigilance, there was nonetheless an increase in the number of people willing to test the law. The new profession of long-distance truck driver, for example, facilitated the transportation of drugs from drug-producing areas of southeast Asia through southern China to Hong Kong, from where it could reach a wide international market. Drugs also flowed from Afghanistan and Pakistan into western China. A quantity of hard drugs like heroin remained in China to feed local demand, but most of the drug shipments made their way to coastal cities for transport overseas.

Drugs were not the only commodity trafficked. As China's economy raised expectations for a better life, it became more difficult for men in poorer villages to find a wife. To fill this need, kidnappers lured young country girls recently arrived in the cities with promises of good jobs. Instead of jobs, however, the girls would be threatened and intimidated into accepting as a husband a man who might pay as much as 8,000 *yuan* (US$1000) for a kidnapped 'bride'. Laws forbidding this practice included stiff penalties, but despite the punishments the practice continued. As long as opportunities for good jobs in rural areas remain scarce, girls will continue to travel to the city and risk capture by such predators.

Related to cases of female exploitation is an increase in prostitution. Virtually eliminated in the Maoist period, this profession quickly re-emerged with the increase in freedom of movement and increasing urban affluence. Penalties can be severe, but the temptation to make what some young women see as 'easy money' draws young women to take the risks involved. Increasingly, the risks are considerable, as the rate of AIDS cases soared toward the end of the 1990s to an estimated 600,000. Infected blood collected by private companies has also been identified as the source of numerous infections, even in some predominantly rural areas of provinces like Henan and Shaanxi. Adequate medical care and counseling have yet to make their way into some of the most-badly hit communities.

While drugs and trafficking in women clearly represent a threat to some segments of Chinese society, of greatest concern to all groups was the increase in corruption among Chinese officials. Under the old Maoist system, not only were the amounts of money an individual official controlled much less than during the reform era, but also the kind of lifestyle money could buy at that time was hardly opulent. With the advent of the economic reforms, opportunities quickly expanded, and many officials, on fixed wages that soon left them economically behind, succumbed to temptation. In some instances, an official simply looked the other way. Far more serious were economic crimes that included the embezzling of millions of *yuan* from state enterprises. The greatest public opprobrium was reserved for officials at the very top of the Party structure who used their positions to enrich themselves and their relatives. The arrests and trials of such individuals were clearly intended to send a message to those lower down the ladder that such behavior would not be tolerated. As of 2000, however, such crimes continued to be reported in the Chinese press, suggesting that the lure of wealth remained seductive.

The authorities found crime a challenge. But they also paid close attention to the emergence of popular religion in the reform era. The presence of a growing foreign business community and an increasing number of foreign journalists resident in the county meant that China's policy on religion was opened to international examination and, as discussed below, the issue of religious freedom continued to draw world-wide attention.

RELIGIOUS POLICY

Because the Communist movement is aetheist, Chinese constitutions have made a point of stressing that while there is freedom of religion in China, citizens have the right to believe or not to believe in any religion. Religion is invariably referred to as 'backward' and a form of 'superstition' which belongs to the past and not to present-day, modern China. Officially, five major religions are legally allowed to practice: Buddhism, Daoism (Taoism),

Islam, Catholicism and Protestantism, each of which has official spokes-persons recognized by the government. These individuals are responsible for any activities among their adherents. As a result of this 'watch-dog' status, the leaders of the officially-recognized religions are seen by many as mere cyphers. Certainly the need to be accountable to the government makes the position of religious leaders very difficult.

Since 1949, policy toward religion has reflected the political climate. Thus, the relative tolerance of the 1950s gave way to the extreme suppression of all religious belief in the period of the Cultural Revolution. Young Red Guards, born after the 1949 liberation, participated in a widespread onslaught against religious sites, defacing what they could not totally destroy. It seemed that all religion would be obliterated in the process.

However, with the advent of the reform era, policy shifted once more. Accusations against religous leaders were withdrawn and a measure of freedom was accorded to religious institutions. In some cases where damage to religious structures had been extreme, money was provided for rebuilding churches, mosques, and temples. In particular, historically important Buddhist sites were cleaned and repaired at public expense. Muslim sites have also been restored, some with government funds and others with support only from the members of the affected congregation.

Christianity, in particular, suffered under the constraints noted above, but difficulties that attended its practice were more profound and stemmed from different roots. As a Western import, Christianity was closely associated with the old unequal treaty system of the nineteenth century. Missionaries of the twentieth century sought to overcome residual antipathy toward their religion through activities related to the 'social gospel' movement which emphasized educational and medical services as an aspect of their ministry in China. But Communist attitudes toward missionaries and their Chinese converts led to their attacking Christian groups in the 1920s and 1930s and, not surprisingly, this enmity continued and intensified with the CCP victory. Only those members of the Christian church willing to place themselves under Party supervision could practice their religion publicly.

The advent of the reform era allowed Chinese Christians to resume religious activities more openly. Churches in major coastal cities re-opened first, largely because of the increasing numbers of foreigners residing in Shanghai, Beijing and Guangzhou. Some church buildings that had been confiscated and used for other purposes once again became houses of worship, although the elderly predominated in most congregations.

Protestant churches in general fared better than Roman Catholic ones. The latter remained in a difficult position because of the requirement of the government that priests' first loyalty be to China, not the Pope. Those refusing to accept this were not allowed to represent Catholicism; as of 2000, a number of priests remained in prison for refusal to accept this 'patriotic' official policy [*Doc. 16*]. In contrast, Protestant groups operated with comparative freedom. Western Protestant missionaries developed new methods of proselytizing: dedicated Protestant Christians simply went to China to work, often as teachers, and used the opportunity of friendship with local people to introduce Christianity, holding religious services in private homes. The government periodically cracks down on those 'foreigners' believed to be active missionaries, but the often young and determined Western Christians are willing to teach for low pay and are therefore tolerated within certain limits.

Even religious movements that claimed traditional Chinese rather than foreign roots have difficulty. In the 1980s, revivals of quasi-religious practices such as *qigong* were at first widely tolerated. This ancient practice emphasized the cultivation of good health through breathing and physical exercises as well as meditation. However, a modern variant of this old form, called *Falungong* (variously translated as the Law of the Wheel or Buddhist Law), made itself unwelcome, despite its seemingly innocuous system of belief. Its leaders promised not only good health and the ability to defeat diseases such as cancer, but also spiritual salvation and even world peace through its practices. Because of its large membership, estimated by some observers to be as high as 10 million, and its public practice of meditation techniques, the CCP viewed its members as trouble-makers. In April 1999, some 10,000 members gathered for a silent demonstration in front of the gates of Zhongnanhai, the Beijing enclave housing the top CCP leadership, to protest against the detention of some of their fellow believers. When this and other demonstrations in the capital were suppressed, *Falungong* members in other cities staged their own silent but nonetheless, for the government, embarassingly public demonstrations. On 22 July 1999, the organization was declared illegal and all public and private observance of its rituals banned. The leading figure associated with the movement, Li Hongzhi, who had left for the United States sometime earlier, was denounced as a criminal. Neither that accusation nor the official ban stopped members from practicing their religion, and therefore demonstrations and arrests continued.

While the general population could follow their religious beliefs within the limits described above, CCP members were expected to end any religious affiliation. In minority areas in particular, the government was adamant in requiring formerly Muslim or Buddhist cadres to repudiate their beliefs. In some cases, instruction in atheism was offered to minority cadre [*Doc. 17*]. But because religion was seen by many minority groups as an important component of their national identity, leading cadres who no longer followed their people's religious practices risked isolating themselves from the people they were supposed to represent. This remains a dilemma for the new generation of leaders in China's autonomous regions.

EQUITY IN EDUCATION

One goal of the PRC was to provide education for all its citizens. Efforts began in the 1950s, but were interrupted by economic and political campaigns. Nonetheless, progress was made in reducing the rate of adult illiteracy and in providing a primary school education to both boys and girls. By 1980, millions of young Chinese had been given the chance to improve their lives through greater educational opportunities.

Officially, China established compulsory education for those aged from 7 to17. Unofficially, however, many students who began elementary school never finished, in part because during the reform period schools of all levels began assessing fees. Although the amounts charged were very modest by Western standards, the fact that their child's education would cost the family money has meant that poorer families tended to remove their children – usually daughters – from school after only a few years of education. The government's pride in the often-quoted statistic that 90% or more of China's children attend primary school does not indicate the number which does not finish. In urban areas, a child is most likely to have 12 years of schooling, but the cost of going to a good middle and high school can be astronomical. For example, in northeastern Chinese cities, a family could pay several thousand American dollars for a year of high school education in a highly-regarded 'key' school. Even more modest middle and high schools charge fees that some families find beyond their means. Although it is difficult to locate statistics on the numbers entering and completing levels of schooling, it appears that the new system is creating a new, educated elite, with new expectations on the part of both the parents and the student for future earnings and status. However, if the issue of equal access to education, in rural and urban areas as well as for males and females, is not addressed, the disparity between those with and without good prospects for economic success can only increase.

The number of Chinese students studying abroad gradually increased as families earning money in the new economy found ways to fund a son or daughter with the right qualifications. Most went for graduate-level training, which was not available at most Chinese universities until the late 1980s. A small number of these students returned to China where family ties and business opportunities provide incentive. The majority, however, chose not to return, often because of a lack of work in the area of their graduate training but also because of a continuing wariness over their prospects in China.

THE CHALLENGE OF EMPLOYMENT AND THE 'FLOATING POPULATION'

During Mao's lifetime, employment was determined by the government. The communes, intended to provide security to all rural residents, absorbed millions of farmers and relocated urban workers. Cities were not accessible to rural residents as the government maintained a strict system of registration which did not allow individuals to change their place of residence except in very specific circumstances. Even marriage to someone with urban residency rights did not automatically allow a rural resident to move. The CCP's goal was to prevent the emergence of huge conurbations – and the many problems associated with highly concentrated urban populations.

The reform era changed this system. As farm families began to lease land for their own crops and explore sideline production, families sought opportunities for maximizing their income. One means by which to do this was to allow the men in the family to seek occasional work in town to augment the family income. By the 1990s, young men from many of China's rural areas traveled in search of seasonal work, joining what has come to be called the 'floating population'. Initially, men traveled for seasonal agricultural or construction work, but as demand rose for these workers, the ranks of men leaving the countryside grew. Because they were 'temporary' workers, the usual permit system did not apply. Many of these workers were housed in temporary shelters on the work sites of new hotels and apartment buildings in towns and cities across China. When a project finished, the men moved on to the next construction site.

The floating population was blamed for many things. Police sought suspects of petty crimes in the workers' shelters; local residents blamed them for fighting and generally misbehaving. When women joined the ranks, they, too, were viewed as being trouble-makers. As these women were also beyond the control of their village family planning committee, officials saw them as potential violators of the one-child policy, although there are no statistics to indicate that this was so. Overall, these seasonal laborers are the key component of the work force that makes possible the rapid construction of new buildings and roadways in China, and despite the sometimes harsh conditions they have endured, the number of workers in this 'free' labor population continued to grow in 2000.

During the 1990s China also witnessed another new phenomenon. As pressure increased on state-run enterprises to make profits not losses, workers were laid off in an effort to gain control of company finances. To make room for younger workers and reduce unemployment rates, government and businesses encouraged women to retire at the age of 50; retirement for women was mandatory at the age of 55. While workers understood the rationale behind this, losing one full-time worker's income caused considerable financial difficulties for families that relied on two incomes to maintain a relatively stable lifestyle. For men who were abruptly laid off, there was little or no unemployment insurance to support their families; those on government pensions could not survive on the small amounts allotted each month. People who had been taught to expect that the government would provide a life-long job now saw their own and their family's future jeopardized by the new economic system.

The numbers of disaffected and unemployed workers grew throughout the 1990s. Northeastern China was hit particularly hard, as this region had a large number of industrial and manufacturing cities reliant on government-owned enterprises. The younger and more enterprising among those laid off joined the 'floating population' but others were unable to do so, because of age or family responsibilities. With no means of livelihood available, many unemployed workers staged demonstrations and demanded that the government provide assistance. Efforts were made to help some individuals, but the problem was not alleviated. The issue of employment for millions of Chinese remained a major threat to the continuing stability of the country in 2000. The government's reliance on China's fast-paced economic reforms to absorb excess labor in the long run offers little comfort to those still seeking a means to support themselves and their families.

All the issues raised above constitute major challenges to the government for the next decades of China's transformation. To meet these challenges, the CCP hopes to foster not only a strong economy – their ultimate answer to all the above woes – but also a new generation that takes pride in their homeland and its accomplishments. The vehicle by which to accomplish this is no longer the old ideology of Marxism–Leninism–Maoism, although those teachings remain officially sacrosanct. Instead, the CCP seeks to encourage a new nationalism in China's population as part of its solution of galvanizing public support, as discussed below.

CHINA'S NEW NATIONALISM

Despite the problems outlined above, which clearly constitute pressing issues for China's government and the CCP, the PRC's new prosperity has also engendered a growing pride in the country's achievements. The lack of full religious freedom and the persistence of what are seen in the West as human rights abuses worry some Chinese but, on the other hand, many also see these as a relatively small price to pay for the opportunities now available as a result of the economic reforms. The chance to build a good life for one's family and pride in what the Chinese people have accomplished both contribute to the spread of a new kind of Chinese nationalism.

Criticism of China by Western nations not only contributed to this new nationalism, but it also brought out a defensive posture that the government has used to good effect. In 1995–96, several influential publications appeared on the theme of a strong and powerful China that deserves respect from foreign states rather than heavy-handed criticism. Although the readership of these works was largely male and urban, the ideas they expressed showed how much some young intellectuals had changed in the short period since the events at Tiananmen Square. One of these books, *Megatrends China* (*Zhongguo daqushi*), included articles originally published by the State Statistics Bureau. The unifying theme of the articles was American efforts to contain China and thereby limit its growth, both domestic and international. America's constant attacks on China's human rights record was presented as just one example of how the United States interferes in China's domestic affairs.

While government agencies could be expected to author such views, another nationalistic salvo came from five young men of the Tiananmen Square generation. Their book, famous under its English title as *A China that Can Say No*, became a Chinese bestseller in the summer of 1996. The authors asserted that Western countries, particularly the United States and Great Britain, opposed China's economic and political clout and therefore sought to dictate China's domestic policy. They portrayed opposition to Beijing's bid to host the Olympic Games and America's hard bargaining over trade issues as part of a conspiracy to dominate and humiliate China. While Chinese intellectuals may have been unimpressed with the extreme nationalist rhetoric, many Chinese supported its anti-Western sentiments and its nationalistic agenda.

Another example of this new trend came a decade after Tiananmen Square when a new generation of students and young Beijingers participated in a different kind of demonstration, this time in support of their country. Following America's bombing of the Chinese embassy in Belgrade during the days of warfare in the Balkans, protestors threw stones and chanted anti-American slogans as they marched through Beijing's diplomatic quarter in May 1999. Pride in the achievements of their country over a remarkably short time-span of two decades gave this new generation a sense of national awareness that not only measured China in comparison to the recent past, but also in terms of its international standing.

By the year 2000, there was a generation that had only known the reform era and its relative prosperity and openness. Despite the unequal distribution of incomes, opportunities to earn money and control one's economic life were eagerly embraced as individuals and families chose to *xia hai*, or 'jump into the sea' of the new economy and make it on their own. Urban residents under the age of 30 could choose from a growing number of options for education and employment, and many took pride in the changes that had brought China back to relative economic prosperity [*Doc. 18*].

By the end of the 1990s, even the youthful student leaders of the 1989 Beijing Spring had moved on. Some had suffered greatly for their roles in the student movement, but others now embraced some of the same economically-driven agendas as did other Chinese of their generation. Among those who suffered the most was Wang Dan, the soft-spoken leader of the early phase of the student occupation of Tiananmen Square, who initially left China but then chose to return, as a result of which he was forced to endure time in prison for his role in what the government viewed as a 'counter-revolutionary' movement. In 1998 he was released on medical grounds after serving a total of seven years. He arrived in the United States where he became a graduate student in history at Harvard University. Wuerkaixi, the most outspoken and irreverent of the young men who had demanded dialogue with top government officials in May of 1989, also fled China in the aftermath of the Tiananmen Square shootings. However, after some years in the United States, he returned to Asia, married a young Chinese woman from Taiwan and went into business there. During an interview given in 1999, he spoke of the naivete of the students and of how they had collectively miscalculated the depth of discontent in 1989 China. Chai Ling, the most visible of the young women leaders of the student movement, made the most dramatic change. In China, she was a graduate student, married to a fellow activist, Feng Congde. Both were the children of doctors and had, therefore, suffered during the period of the Cultural Revolution as offspring of the 'stinking intellectual' class. At the time of Beijing Spring, Chai Ling had already applied to go to the United States for graduate study. After 4 June 1989, she was smuggled out of China and arrived in the United States in 1990. By 1996, she was living in Cambridge, Massachusetts and working on her MBA at the Harvard Business School. Divorced and leading a distinctly American lifestyle, in 1999 she became chief executive officer of an internet company, backed by major American corporate interests. Her success in the United States, and her frequent trips to Taiwan to criticize the CCP, led some to label her an opportunist. Certainly, like other prominent young leaders of Beijing Spring, she had moved on, far from the days in which a stunning act of violence ended a movement whose time had not yet come.

Whatever her personal motivations, Chai Ling's career path was not unlike that hoped for by many of China's younger generation at the end of the twentieth century. Economic success was the new focus of youthful ambitions, not a high post in the government or Party. Civic-minded individuals turned to their careers, and as they prospered, they gained a share in supporting the system that made their prosperity possible. For its part, the CCP continued to emphasize the importance of economic growth and pride in China, as well as a national commitment to making China a strong economic and political power. Mao's words of 1 October 1949 still carried great power: the Chinese people, he said, had stood up. The rhetoric of the 1990s affirmed that this, indeed, was the case.

Although the problems which have accompanied the reforms remain a source of concern, China's new prosperity has also generated a new nationalism among those who will lead the country in the twenty-first century. As long as political stability and economic growth are maintained, it appears that many Chinese will continue to accept these in lieu of political accountability in the short term.

CHAPTER EIGHT

CHINA AND THE WORLD

CHINA, EUROPE AND THE USA

The transformation of China from a struggling, third-world country to a leading economic power required a re-examination of China's place in the world by other governments. At the beginning of China's shift to a market economy and the reforms of the Deng period, the United States finally extended official recognition to China in 1979. De-recognition of Taiwan's Nationalist government as the only government of China came on the heels of the unsuccessful American intervention in Viet Nam, and signaled the beginning of a re-ordering of power structures in Asia.

In the 1980s, the United Kingdom recognized China's new position as a powerful, emerging state by signing the 1984 agreement to return Hong Kong, part of which (Hong Kong Island) was ceded in perpetuity to England in the treaty settlements of the mid-nineteenth century. By returning the entirety of the Hong Kong area in 1997, the UK re-configured its relationship with China as nation-to-nation, rather than Western power to third-world state. The re-integration of the former colony with China provided the CCP with an opportunity to show its ability to reunite peacefully the capitalist enclave of the south with its own increasingly diversified economic system. Hong Kong's strong economy and nascent democratic forms did not collapse, as some predicted, but instead remained an important component of south China's economic engine.

The return of Hong Kong was followed by the recovery of Macao, a colony of Portugal since 1557. The Portuguese had, in fact, sought to return the small European town on the South China Sea in 1976, but at that time China had not been prepared to begin the negotiations for a settlement. It was thus in 1999, at the very end of the twentieth century, that Macao also reverted to Chinese control. The unique Macanese society quietly began its new existence as a Special Administrative Region which, like Hong Kong, was protected from inundation by Chinese from elsewhere in the PRC by rules that continued to restrict travel in and out of the two former colonies.

Although China's trading relations with countries around the globe expanded rapidly in the reform era, Western states' concerns with human rights issues in China stirred controversy over granting China normal trading privileges and entrance into world trade organizations. In the United States and Great Britain, supporters of Tibetan independence, Christian activists, and anti-abortion groups worked against the normalization of trade relations, while major corporations put increasing pressure on the American government for an end to the annual review of China's trading status.

In 2000, the United States' decision to grant China 'permanent normal trade relations' (PNTR) status confirmed China's importance as a world economic power, and set the stage for an era of more equitable trade relations between the two states. This change ended the American practice of holding trade privileges hostage to human rights issues and the vagaries of American politics. It also paved the way for China's entry into the World Trade Organization (WTO), making China an equal partner in international trade. As such, China will also become subject to WTO regulations and practices, which may prove to be further incentives for both political and economic change in twenty-first-century China.

The shifting nature of American relations with China came into focus early in the administration of President George W. Bush when an American surveillance plane made a forced landing on the island of Hainan, off China's southern coast, on 1 April 2001. Each side provided its own account of what appeared to be an accidental collision between the slow-moving American aeroplane and a Chinese fighter plane which crashed, killing its pilot, as a result of the encounter. After a series of talks and diplomatic maneuvering on both sides, the American crew was allowed to return to the United States. The aeroplane was later dismantled and returned. For China, its ability to 'say no' was impressed upon the United States as well as its own citizenry, whose growing nationalism was fed by American reluctance to offer an apology or, initially, even condolences for the death of the Chinese pilot, who was the only casualty. Nonetheless, while the political posturing continued on both sides, business transactions also continued as usual, strengthening some observers' belief that economics will ultimately outweigh any political issues that may arise between the two nations, at least in the immediate future [*Doc. 19*].

CHINA AND TAIWAN

Just as China itself continued to undergo dramatic changes, Taiwan also felt the shifting expectations of its own citizens. In 2000, the Nationalist Party (Guomindang) lost its half-century-long hold on the presidency of Taiwan. Ever since their defeat in 1948–49 by the CCP, the Nationalists dominated

Taiwan, the island state where American ally Jiang Jieshi (Chiang Kai-shek) served as president from 1950 until his death in 1975, with American military support to buoy his claim to leadership of all China. His son, Jiang Jingguo (Chiang Ching-kuo) followed him, and successfully weathered the de-recognition of Taiwan by the United States in 1979 as well as the emergence of an opposition political party, the Democratic Progressive Party (DPP), which openly advocated the independence of the island. Reluctantly, the Nationalists extended recognition to the DPP but government control of Taiwan media limited the new party's impact. When Jiang Jingguo died, still in office in 1988, leadership passed to the vice president, Taiwan-born and American-educated Li Denghui (Lee Teng-hui), who continued the Nationalist policies he inherited.

However, Taiwan's strong economy and high standard of living were not enough to ensure a continued Nationalist hold on the presidency. In 2000, the Nationalist Party, weakened by internal divisions, lost to the DPP candidate, Chen Shuibian. The new president was sworn into office that May. Taiwan's election was not only ground-breaking in its defeat of the Nationalists, it also placed a woman in the second highest office in the land. The new vice president was Annette Lu, whose credentials included long years of opposition to the Nationalists [see *Doc. 20*, written by Vice President Lu]. Although Chen's election was a remarkable event, the Nationalists retained control of Taiwan's legislature with 55% of the seats compared to the DPP's 31%.

China's opposition to Chen Shuibian was made clear in the run-up to the March 2000 election. Because Chen was known as an advocate for Taiwan independence, China repeated its conviction that Tawian was a Chinese province and that its future lay with China. And just as it had done prior to the 1996 elections, the CCP issued threatening warnings about what might happen in the future should Chen win. Despite the heated rhetoric, both sides defused the situation by moderating their tones after the election. Chen issued a call for friendly ties with China and spoke of future direct transport and communication links. China remained cool to Taiwan's overtures, but at the same time continued to welcome Taiwan businesses. Plans for direct trade across the Taiwan Straits were quietly announced at the end of 2001, and promises to be the first of proposed steps to ease trade between the two. Both governments have everything to gain from closer ties, and considering the US$30 billion Taiwan investors have put into China since the late 1980s, the future direction of talks across the Taiwan Straits will clearly have economic as well as political agendas in mind.

CHINA AS A REGIONAL POWER

While Communism in the West disappeared as a political force with the fall of the Berlin Wall and the collapse of the USSR, it retained a position of power in Asia. On China's own periphery, Viet Nam and North Korea remained communist states. Viet Nam's recovery from long years of warfare in the 1960s and 1970s was relatively rapid, and trade between China and Viet Nam soon thrived. North Korea, on the other hand, increasingly suffered from its own self-imposed isolation. The presence of 36,000 American troops in South Viet Nam provided a strong rationale for China to continue its own relationship with North Korea. In the late 1990s, however, the small communist state suffered from severe famine. North Koreans swarmed across the border to search for food in northeastern China. This development contributed to North Korea opening its doors far enough to admit aid from international relief organizations. More dramatic was the first meeting, in 2000, between President Kim Dae Jung of South Korea and Kim Jong Il of North Korea. Visits by selected groups of South Koreans to the North followed, auguring well for future contact between the two long-estranged peoples.

China's trading relations with Japan continued to develop, interrupted by the Asian crisis of 1997 which hurt Japan's economy far more than China's. The Japanese recovery began only at the end of the decade, while China, even during the worst of the crisis, continued to enjoy an economy that expanded at 8% per annum. Nonetheless, technological advice and a huge tourism industry catering to Japanese tourists meant that relations with Japan remained important to China, despite the periodic denunciation of Japan for its record in China during the Second World War, which remained an open wound for the generation touched by those events.

In 1991, China faced the issue of establishing diplomatic relations with new neighbors in Central Asia. Abruptly independent from Russian dominance, the new states of Kazakhstan, Kyrgyzstan, and Tajikistan now shared China's long northwestern border. The PRC moved quickly to open talks with these new states, most of which were led by men who owed their positions of power to the former USSR. New agreements replaced the former Sino-Soviet arrangements and enhanced the amount of cross-border trade. China's concern over its own Muslim populations prompted additional agreements that were intended to limit agitation by representatives of China's Muslim communities for greater rights and political autonomy. Despite such assurances, however, the predominantly Muslim region of Xinjiang continued to experience considerable unrest, suggesting that China's internal problems with minorities will not be resolved simply through agreements with neighboring states [*Doc. 21*].

Although some observers cite the dwindling number of communist states as proof of the out-moded appeal of Marxism in the twenty-first century, a Maoist group in Nepal, a country which shares a long border with Tibet, suggests that the appeal of both Marxism and Maoism remains in some of the world's poorest nations. This insurgency, which became increasingly violent in 1999–2000, may pose a new dilemma to the leaders of China, a country which, in practice, is leaving behind many of the socialist goals which this Nepalese group now espouses.

Over the course of the last half of the twentieth century, China has moved from its position as an isolated, marginal state preoccupied with domestic socialist change and defense of its immediate borders, to that of a powerful player in Asia's regional affairs and an increasingly outspoken and assertive player in international politics. This rapid shift has raised concerns among some who see China as a new, emergent threat that could replace the USSR as the second great superpower. The integration of China into the WTO and other international bodies suggests that China will, indeed, play an ever-increasing international role, but it does not follow that China's relationship with other states, particularly the United States and those in Europe, need follow a path of growing antagonism or confrontation. Whether international affairs move toward greater cooperation and understanding will ultimately depend not only on China or the United States, but on the determination of all nations to use dialogue and diplomacy in resolving their differences.

PART THREE   ASSESSING CHINA'S HALF-CENTURY UNDER THE CCP

CHAPTER NINE

CONCLUSIONS

As China moves into the twenty-first century, the imprint of the past 50 years clearly remains. An examination of the accomplishments and shortcomings of the CCP-led government reveals, on the one hand, the enormity of the challenges the Party faced in its early years as the sole authority in China, as well as the failure of the Maoist leaders to resolve issues within the Party leadership and to provide stable economic development. The contrast between the Maoist period and the reform era which followed provides an opportunity to assess a half-century of CCP leadership.

Whether China's socialist experiment under revolutionary leader Mao was more failure than success remains a topic of scholarly discussion. Most would agree that Mao led China out of an era of national division and toward an egalitarian society with a relatively narrow gap between the wealthiest and poorest groups of Chinese. But most would also agree that the promised new society, built on loyalty to the Party and its socialist ideals, not only never materialized but instead gave rise to a new bureaucratic elite that wielded unquestioned power and enjoyed prerogatives not available to the ordinary citizen. While the old landlord elite was gone, the new elite followed in the time-worn footsteps of those who, for many centuries past, led the people but also cultivated personal and familial benefits in the process. The Maoist system was not able to prevent this, nor was it able to forestall the concentration of great power in the hands of a small gerontocracy which managed to maintain its hold over Chinese society.

Mao's stature as a leader of the Chinese people has also been marred by the ill-considered policies of the Great Leap Forward and the Cultural Revolution. Suffering inflicted through blind obedience to ideals that were poorly understood by either the rural cadres ordering foolish agricultural practices or by teenage Red Guards inflicting pain on their elders was ultimately the responsibility of Mao and his hand-picked supporters. Their responsibility for bringing disaster to millions of people cannot be forgotten in any assessment of either Mao or the CCP as a whole.

Following Mao's death in 1976, the CCP shifted course dramatically. The Dengist reform policies rejuvenated a stagnant economy and unleashed the energies of ordinary men and women who quickly embraced the new opportunities in rural and urban China. While the average incomes of Chinese people remained far below those of their counterparts in Hong Kong or Taiwan, the standard of living improved enormously. Overall economic growth slowed in the late 1990s, but it was still averaging an annual growth of over 7% in 2000–01. The result was a GDP of US$4.8 trillion, and a per capita income of US$3,500, the latter figure up from US$250 in less than a decade.

International corporations once more saw China as a land of business opportunity, and although initial profits were not always as expected, that interest remained high in 2000. Skilled workers, without unions to represent their interests, became a key attraction as the work forces of other Asian countries became more expensive in comparison to workers in China. Foreign investment continued to climb, as did the amount provided to China in loans from international lenders such as the World Bank. If stability in the political system can be maintained, China's place in the world economy will continue to strengthen.

The problems of this transformation into a modern economy, as suggested in the preceding chapters, remain a challenge for the country and its one-party system. Younger Chinese may be increasingly patriotic, and ultra-nationalist views may appeal to some, but these trends also face a counter-current in the form of increasing discontent with the government's handling of unemployment, rising crime, and the overall lack of government accountability. The CCP itself continued to keep its highest echelon activities shrouded in secrecy, and while men in top Party posts are generations removed from the 'revolutionaries' who fought against Jiang Jieshi, all adhere to established practices that remain deeply entrenched. Without a shift to greater transparency and public discussion of policies, the CCP may find it difficult to maintain its credibility as a party capable of leading a modern state.

Already, some groups feel the problems of reform more acutely than others. For China's women, there are special problems in this 'get rich quick' era. Today, most women work, but jobs for women are disproportionately in the low-paid sectors of the economy. Urban women complain of the 'double burden' of housework and a job, as well as primary responsibility for their child. In rural areas, the tendency for farming families to rely on women as the primary labor force, while the men seek other, better-paid and higher-status employment, means that rural women are often left with the responsibility of both the farm work and all family matters. On average, girls still receive fewer years of education and are therefore at a disadvantage in seeking better employment opportunities. The return of prostitution and trafficking in women are further instances of the negative impact of the reforms on China's women. New laws have been enacted to address some of these issues, but enforcement remains a problem.

Among China's minority groups, there is also a mixed response to China's new policies. On the one hand, like other areas of China, the minority regions have seen their economies grow and facilities for health care and education improve. On the other hand, there has been an increase in complaints over Chinese domination in economic and cultural affairs. In Xinjiang, for example, local people complain that new economic development benefits Han newcomers and the Central Government, but not them. The practice of encouraging more Chinese to move out to the northwest is seen by some as a plot to marginalize and disenfranchise Uighurs in their own autonomous region. In reply to such charges, the Chinese press accuses outside forces of fomenting discontent and fostering 'separatist' ideas among the Uighurs, whose Muslim faith and history of antagonistic relations with the Chinese continue to divide them from the Han majority [*Doc. 21*]. Ironically, just as Chinese nationalism has spread among some Han Chinese, Uighur nationalism has also emerged as a potent local force with which the Chinese government must contend. Keeping the borders open to the outside while trying to contain the spread of ideas and attitudes contrary to the goals of the CCP may prove a difficult balancing act for the Central Government as it implements plans to develop the natural resources of Xinjiang and other minority regions.

In many ways the questions facing China today reflect the country's long struggle to find a political form that meets both the economic and social needs of all its people – its urban and rural minority and majority, male and female citizens. Whether that future form includes only the CCP – or a Western-style multiparty system – will largely depend on the CCP's ability to resolve the country's major problems and, at the same time, ensure an acceptable standard of living for the majority of the people. As Taiwan's own long struggle toward a more accountable government has shown, the Chinese people's own ability and tenacity are the single greatest asset China has as it moves through the twenty-first century.

PART FOUR DOCUMENTS

One of the first laws passed by the new government was the Marriage Law which made women the legal equals of men. It was promulgated on 1 May 1950.

GENERAL PRINCIPLES:

Article 1. The arbitrary and compulsory feudal marriage system, the supremacy of man over woman, and disregard of the interests of children is abolished.

The new democratic marriage system, which is based on the free choice of partners, on monogamy, on equal rights for both sexes, and on the protection of the lawful interests of women and children, is put into effect.

Article 2. Bigamy, concubinage, child betrothal, interference in the remarriage of widows, and the exaction of money or gifts in connection with marriages, are prohibited.

THE MARRIAGE CONTRACT

Article 3. Marriage is based upon the complete willingness of the two parties. Neither party shall use compulsion and no third party is allowed to interfere.

Article 4. A marriage can be contracted only after the man reaches twenty years of age and the woman eighteen years of age. ...

RIGHTS AND DUTIES OF HUSBAND AND WIFE

Article 7. Husband and wife are companions living together and enjoy equal status in the home.

Article 8. Husband and wife are in duty bound to love, respect, assist and look after each other, to live in harmony, to engage in productive work, to care for their children, and to strive jointly for the welfare of the family and for the building up of the new society.

Article 9. Both husband and wife have the right to use free choice of occupation and free participation in work or in social activities. ...

DIVORCE

Article 17. Divorce is granted when the husband and wife both desire it. In the event of the husband or the wife alone insisting upon divorce, it may be granted only when mediation by the district people's government and the judicial organ has failed to bring about a reconciliation. ...

Article 18. The husband is not allowed to apply for a divorce when his wife is pregnant, and may apply for divorce only one year after the birth of the child. In the case of a woman applying for divorce, this restriction does not apply. ...

MAINTENANCE AND EDUCATION OF CHILDREN AFTER DIVORCE

Article 20. The blood ties between parents and children are not ended by the divorce of the parents. No matter whether the father or the mother has custody of the children, they remain the children of both parties.

After divorce, both parents continue to have the duty to support and educate their children.

After divorce, the guiding principle is to allow the mother to have the custody of a breast-fed infant. After the weaning of the child, if a dispute arises between the two parties over the guardianship and an agreement cannot be reached, the people's court should render a decision in accordance with the interests of the child.

Article 21. If, after the divorce, the mother is given custody of a child, the father is responsible for the whole or part of the necessary cost of maintenance and education of the child. Both parties should reach an agreement regarding the amount and the duration of such maintenance and education. Lacking such an agreement, the people's court should render a decision.

Kay Ann Johnson, *Women, the Family and Peasant Revolution in China* (Chicago: University
of Chicago Press, 1983), pp. 235–9. (From a 1950 Chinese government pamphlet
issued in Beijing.)

DOCUMENT 2   **THE 17-POINT AGREEMENT BETWEEN TIBET AND CHINA**

On 23 May 1951, representatives of the PRC and the Dalai Lama signed the 'Agreement on Measures for the Peaceful Liberation of Tibet', also known as the '17-Point Agreement'. This document set out the terms for the peaceful merging of Tibet with the new PRC. The following is a Chinese summary of the content of the agreement which was abrogated by both sides in 1959.

The important content [of the agreement] was as follows: expel imperialist aggressors from Tibet; assist the Chinese People's Liberation Army to enter Tibet [in order to] strengthen border defense; merge all of Tibet's local government departments with the central people's government departments; put into practice minority district governments or autonomous governments under the united leadership of the CCP and the central people's government; reform Tibet's social system; change the Tibetan military step by step; expand Tibetan government, economy and culture; improve the people's livelihood; and so on.

In signing this agreement, Tibetans threw off forever imperialist aggression and returned to the motherland, thereby consolidating the unity of the motherland.

Shi Zhengdyi, ed., *Minzu Cidian* [*Dictionary of the Nationalities*] (Chengdu, Sichuan: Sichuan minzu chubanshe, 1984), p. 44. Translated by Linda Benson.

DOCUMENT 3   THE TIBETAN VIEW OF THE 17-POINT AGREEMENT

In 1962, the Dalai Lama published his memoirs in which he recounted the circumstances and the content of the 17-Point Agreement. The following selection is his summary of the content and what it meant to the Tibetans.

Neither I nor my government were told that an agreement had been signed. We first came to know of it from a broadcast which Nagbo[1] made on Peking Radio. It was a terrible shock when we heard the terms of it. We were appalled at the mixture of Communist clichés, vainglorious assertions which were completely false, and bold statements which were only partly true. And the terms were far worse and more oppressive than anything we had imagined.

The preamble said that 'over the last one hundred years or more', imperialist forces had penetrated into China and Tibet and 'carried out all kinds of deceptions and provocations', and that 'under such conditions, the Tibetan nationality and people were plunged into the depths of enslavement and suffering'. This was pure nonsense. It admitted that the Chinese government had ordered the 'People's Liberation Army' to march into Tibet. Among the reasons given were that the influence of aggressive imperialist forces in Tibet might be successfully eliminated and that the Tibetan people might be freed and return to the 'big family' of the People's Republic of China.

That was also the subject of Clause One of the agreement: 'The Tibetan people shall unite and drive out imperialist aggressive forces from Tibet. The Tibetan people shall return to the big family of the Motherland – the People's Republic of China.' Reading this, we reflected bitterly that there had been no foreign forces whatever in Tibet since we drove out the last of the Chinese forces in 1912. Clause Two provided that the 'local government of Tibet shall actively assist the People's Liberation Army to enter Tibet and consolidate the national defense'. This in itself went beyond the specific limits we had placed on Ngabo's authority. Clause Eight provided for the absorption of the Tibetan army into the Chinese army. Clause Fourteen deprived Tibet of all authority in external affairs.

In between these clauses, which no Tibetan would ever willingly accept, were others in which the Chinese made many promises: not to alter the existing political system in Tibet; not to alter the status, functions, and powers of the Dalai Lama; to respect the religious beliefs, customs, and habits of the Tibetan people and protect the monasteries; to develop agriculture and improve the people's standard of living; and not to compel the people to accept reforms. But these promises were small comfort beside the fact that we were expected to hand ourselves and our country over to China and cease to exist as a nation. Yet we were helpless. Without friends there was nothing we could do but acquiesce, submit to the Chinese dictates in spite of our strong opposition, and swallow our resentment. We could only hope that the Chinese would keep their side of this forced, one-sided bargain.

---

[1] Nagbo Ngawan Jigme was governor of eastern Tibet in 1950; he was appointed to open negotiations with the new PRC by the Dalai Lama.

Dalai Lama, *My Land and My People* (New York: McGraw Hill, 1962), pp. 88–89.

DOCUMENT 4   'SPEAK BITTERNESS' MEETINGS

As part of the land redistribution process, poor peasants were encouraged to speak out publicly against those who had abused or exploited them. The following selection is a villager's description of how this process worked, as told to William Hinton, author and sinologist. This particular meeting occurred before 1949, in an area already under CCP control, but it was to be duplicated many times all across China in the early 1950s.

When the final struggle began Ching-ho [a local landlord] was faced not only with those hundred accusations but with many many more. Old women who had never spoken in public before stood up to accuse him. Even Li Mao's wife – a woman so pitiable she hardly dared look anyone in the face – shook her fist before his nose and cried out, 'Once I went to glean wheat on your land. But you cursed me and drove me away. Why did you curse me and beat me? And why did you seize the wheat I had already gleaned?' Altogether over 180 opinions were raised. Ching-ho had no answer to any of them. He stood there with his head bowed. We asked him whether the accusations were false or true. He said they were all true. When the committee of our Association met to figure up what he owed, it came to 400 bags of milled grain, not coarse grain.

That evening all the people went to Ching-ho's courtyard to help take over his property. It was very cold that night so we built bonfires and the flames shot up toward the stars. It was very beautiful. We went in to register his grain and altogether found but 200 bags of unmilled millet – only a quarter of what he owed us. Right then and there we decided to call another meeting. People all said he must have a lot of silver dollars – they thought of the wine plant, and the pigs he raised on the distillers' grains, and the North Temple Society and the Confucius Association.

We called him out of the house and asked him what he intended to do since the grain was not nearly enough. He said, 'I have land and house.'

'But all this is not enough,' shouted the people. So then we began to beat him. Finally he said, 'I have 40 silver dollars under the *k'ang*.' We went in and dug it up. The money stirred up everyone. We beat him again. He told us where to find another hundred after that. But no one believed that this was the end of his hoard. We beat him again and several militiamen began to heat an iron bar in one of the fires. Then Ching-ho admitted that he had hid 110 silver dollars in militiaman Man-hsi's uncle's home. Man-hsi was very hot-headed. When he heard that his uncle had helped Sheng Ching-ho he got very angry. He ran home and began to beat his father's own brother. We stopped him. We told him, 'Your uncle didn't know it was a crime.' We asked the old man why he had hidden money for Ching-ho and he said, 'No one ever told me anything. I didn't know there was anything wrong in it.' You see, they were relatives and the money had been given to him for safekeeping years before. So Man-hsi finally cooled down. It was a good thing for he was angry enough to beat his uncle to death and he was strong enough to do it.

Altogether we got $500 from Ching-ho that night. By that time the sun was already rising in the eastern sky. We were all tired and hungry, especially the militiamen who had called the people to the meeting, kept guard on Ching-ho's house, and taken an active part in beating Ching-ho and digging for the money. So we decided to eat all the things that Ching-ho had prepared to pass the New Year – a whole crock of dumplings stuffed with pork and peppers and other delicacies. He even had shrimp.

All said, 'In the past we never lived through a happy New Year because he always asked for his rent and interest then and cleaned our houses bare. This time we'll eat what we like,' and everyone ate his fill and didn't even notice the cold.

William Hinton, *Fanshen: A Documentary of Revolution in a Chinese Village* (New York: Random House, 1968), pp. 137–8.

DOCUMENT 5   CHINA'S REGIONAL AUTONOMY SYSTEM

In order to give minority groups a voice in local government, the new Chinese government passed the Program for Enforcement of Nationality Regional Autonomy on 8 August 1952. The following are extracts from the Program.

CHAPTER I. GENERAL PRINCIPLES

Article 1. This program is enacted on the basis of the provisions of Articles 9, 50, 51, 52 and 53 of the People's Political Consultative Conference's [PPCC's] Common Program.

Article 2. All national autonomous districts shall be an inseparable part of the territory of the People's Republic of China. All autonomous organs of the national autonomous districts shall be local state power organs under the unified leadership of the Central People's Government and subject to guidance by the people's governments of superior levels.

Article 3. The PPCC Common Program shall be the general direction for unity and struggle of all nationalities of the People's Republic of China at the present stage, and the people of all national autonomous districts shall proceed along this general path in administering the internal affairs of their own nationalities. ...

CHAPTER III. AUTONOMOUS ORGANS

Article 12. The people's government organs of national autonomous districts shall be formed principally of personnel of national minorities carrying out regional autonomy and shall include an appropriate number of personnel of other national minorities and Han Chinese in the autonomous districts. ...

CHAPTER IV. RIGHTS OF AUTONOMY

Article 15. The autonomous organs of national autonomous districts may adopt the national language commonly used in the autonomous districts as the principal instrument to exercise their authority but, in exercising authority among national minorities not using such language, should adopt the language of the national minorities in question at the same time.

Article 16. The autonomous organs of national autonomous districts may adopt their own national language, both spoken and written, for the development of the cultural and educational work of national minorities. ...

Article 18. Internal reform of national autonomous districts shall be carried out according to the will of the majority of people of national minorities and the leaders having close ties with the people.

Article 19. Under the unified financial system of the state, the autonomous organs of national autonomous districts may, according to the power concerning financial matters of the national autonomous districts as defined by the Central People's Government and governments of superior levels, administer the finance of their own districts. ...

Article 23. Within the scope defined by the laws of the Central People's Government and of governments of superior levels and according to their prescribed rights, the autonomous organs of national autonomous districts may enact their own independent laws and regulations and report them step-by-step to the people's governments of two levels above for approval. ...

CHAPTER VI. GUIDING PRINCIPLES FOR PEOPLE'S GOVERNMENT OF SUPERIOR LEVELS

Article 33. The people's governments of superior levels shall introduce, by appropriate means, advanced experience and conditions of political, economic and cultural construction to the people of autonomous districts. ...

Article 35. The people's governments of superior levels shall educate and assist the people of all nationalities to establish the viewpoint of equality, fraternity, unity and mutual help among all nationalities and shall combat all tendencies of greater nationalism and narrow nationalism.

New China News Agency, 12 August 1952, translated in *Survey of China Mainland Press*,
No. 394, 12–16.

DOCUMENT 6　**POLITICAL CAMPAIGNS OF 1957–58**

During the '100 Flowers Campaign', criticism of the CCP emerged which then became the basis for attacking individuals who had dared to speak up. Some of the criticisms put forward in minority areas are mentioned in the following selection which dates from the end of the Anti-rightist Campaign of 1957–58. The names are romanized in the Wade Giles system, as in the original translation.

Vice Chairman Ts'ui K'e-nan of the Provincial Nationalities Affairs Commission [of Hunan] said at the meeting: These few years our province has established one autonomous *chou* [prefecture] and four autonomous *hsien* [county] in areas where the Tuchia, the Miao, the Tung and the Yao nationalities live collectively. ... Great progress has been made in the various tasks of construction. ...

He pointed out: Rightists among the minority nationalities negated the achievement in the nationality work and exaggerated or even fabricated shortcomings and mistakes, thus basically disagreeing with us on the key issue[s] in the nationality work.

Ts'ui K'e-nan said: The Party's policy is, on the foundation of the socialist system, to consolidate the unity of the motherland and the unity of the various nationalities, so that they may together construct the big socialist family. We advocate the placing of national self-respect and national sentiments under the guidance of the socialist ideology, and their association with class sentiments and the interests of the state. While giving due consideration to national characteristics, we must associate them with the interests of the collective body. The rightists cherish the diametrically opposite view. They insist on placing national sentiments above class sentiments and the interest of the state, putting local interests above collective interests. ... In the various reforms and constructive tasks carried out in minority nationality areas, the help of the Han cadres is essential. But the rightists say that the Han cadres and the Han Communists cannot stand for the interests of the minority nationalities, cannot serve the minority nationalities. They negate the fact that the Communist Party stands for the interests of all nationalities. ...

P'eng Tsu-kuei, deputy chief of the West Hunan Tuchia and Miao autonomous *chou*, said: Rightists P'an Kuang-tan and Hsiang Ta work in collaboration with P'eng P'e and other rightists of the Tuchia nationality. Wearing the cloak of 'attending to the interests of the nationalities' and waving the flag of 'fighting for regional autonomoy for the nationalities,' they carry out activities in an organized and planned manner to create incidents on the issue of regional autonomy for the people of West Hunan, sow discord, and organize landlords, rich peasants, counter-revolutionaries, bad elements, rascals, ruffians and what not into a nuclear sub-committee to expand their reactionary anti-communist, anti-popular and anti-socialist force. ...

On the issue of the relations among the nationalities, the rightists claim that the Communist Party 'favors the Miao and discriminates against the Tuchia,' thereby intending to arouse the discontent of the Tuchia people against the Communist Party and excite mutual suspicions among, and split, the nationalities. ... Thus they try by various means to sabotage the unity among our nationalities.

P'eng Tsu-kuei added: The rightist crimes, having been exposed, arouse the great indignation of all the nationalities in the *chou*. After several months' anti-rightist struggle, the rightists have been isolated from the masses of nationality people.

New China News Agency, 'Hunan Provincial People's Congress Criticizes Local Nationalism', 2 January 1958, translated in *Survey of China Mainland Press*, No. 1689, pp. 20–3.

DOCUMENT 7   RECOLLECTIONS OF THE GREAT LEAP FORWARD

China's peasant-farmers at first supported the Great Leap Forward, but it soon became apparent that the new planting practices were a disaster. In interviews with villagers in south China, the following account was given by local farmers.

They pushed a system of planting called 'Sky Full of Stars' where a field would be so overplanted the seedlings starved each other out. ... The peasants knew it was useless, but there was simply no way to oppose anything, because the orders came from so high above. And if one of our Chen Village cadres protested at commune meetings, he laid himself open to criticisms: 'a rightist, against the revolution.' ... The peasants were ordered to smash their water jars to make them into fertilizer. They said it was stupid, that the jars were just sterile clay, but they had to smash the jars nonetheless. What a mess! Cut rice was left overnight in the fields [and mildewed] while exhausted villagers were ordered off to do other things. The period was called the 'Eat-It-All-Up Period' because people were eating five and six times daily – but there was no harvest that year. Everything had been given to the collective. Nothing was left in the houses. No grain had been stored. People were so hungry they had difficulty sleeping ... some people became ill, and some of the elderly died. Our village became quiet, as if the people were dead.

Anita Chen, Richard Madsen and Jonathan Unger, *Chen Village under Mao and Deng*
(Berkeley, CA: University of California Press, 1992), p. 25.

DOCUMENT 8   A LETTER TO MAO ON THE GREAT LEAP
             FORWARD

This letter by Peng Dehuai pointed out the shortcomings of the Great Leap Forward; despite the truth of Peng's observations, he was removed from all positions of power after this letter was circulated, by Mao, among the top CCP leaders in 1959.

Dear Chairman:
This Lushan Meeting is important. In the discussions in the Northwest Group, I commented on other speakers' remarks several times. Now I am stating, specially for your reference, a number of my views that I have not expressed fully at the group meetings. I may be as straightforward as Zhang Fei, but I possess only his roughness without his tact. Therefore, please consider whether what I am about to write is worth your attention, point out whatever is wrong, and give me your instructions.

... The Great Leap Forward has basically proved the correctness of the General Line for building socialism with greater, quicker, better, and more economical results in a country like ours, hampered by a weak economic foundation and by backward technology and equipment. Not only is this a great success for China, it will also play a long-term positive role in the socialist camp.

But as we can see now, an excessive number of capital construction projects were hastily started in 1958. With part of the funds being dispersed, completion of some essential projects had to be postponed. This is a shortcoming, one caused mainly by lack of experience. Because we did not have a deep enough understanding, we came to be aware of it too late. So we continued with our Great Leap Forward in 1959 instead of putting on the brakes and slowing down our pace accordingly. As a result, imbalances were not corrected in time and new temporary difficulties cropped up. ...

In the nationwide campaign for the production of iron and steel, too many small blast furnaces were built with a waste of material, money, and manpower. This, of course, was a rather big loss. On the other hand, through the campaign we have been able to conduct a preliminary geological survey across the country, train many technicians, temper the vast numbers of cadres and raise their level. Though we paid a steep tuition (we spent over 2,000 million *yuan* to subsidize the effort), there were gains as well as losses in this endeavor.

Considering the above-mentioned points alone, we can say that our achievements have been really great, but we also have quite a few profound lessons to learn. ...

A number of problems that have developed merit attention in regard to our way of thinking and style of work. ... The exaggeration trend has become so common in various areas and departments that reports of unbelievable miracles have appeared in newspapers and magazines to bring a great loss of prestige to the Party. According to what was reported, it seemed that communism was just around the corner, and this turned the heads of many comrades. Extravagance and waste grew in the wake of reports of extra-large grain and cotton harvests and a doubling of iron and steel output. As a result, the autumn harvest was done in a slipshod manner, and costs were not taken into consideration. Though we were poor, we lived as if we were rich.

Patricia Ebrey, ed., *Chinese Civilization: A Sourcebook* (New York: The Free Press, 1981), pp. 436–9.

DOCUMENT 9   'THE LITTLE RED BOOK': QUOTATIONS FROM CHAIRMAN MAO

The following quotations were among those studied diligently by soldiers of the PLA and then by millions of young people who joined the ranks of the Red Guards between 1966–1969.

'The Chinese Communist Party is the core of leadership of the whole Chinese people. Without this core, the cause of socialism cannot be victorious.'

'A revolution is not a dinner party, or writing an essay, or painting a picture, or doing embroidery; it cannot be so refined, so leisurely and gentle, so temperate, kind, courteous, restrained and magnanimous. A revolution is an insurrection, an act of violence by which one class overthrows another.'

'It is an arduous task to ensure a better life for the several hundred million people of China and to build our economically and culturally backward country into a prosperous and powerful one with a high level of culture. And it is precisely in order to be able to shoulder this task more competently and work better together with all non-Party people who are actuated by high ideals and determined to institute reforms that we must conduct rectification movements both now and in the future, and constantly rid ourselves of whatever is wrong.'

'Every Communist must grasp the truth, "Political power grows out of the barrel of a gun".'

'Our principle is that the Party commands the gun, and the gun must never be allowed to command the Party.'

'The people and the people alone, are the motive force in the making of world history.'

'The wealth of society is created by the workers, peasants and working intellectuals. If they take their destiny into their own hands, follow a Marxist–Leninist line and take an active attitude in solving problems instead of evading them, there will be no difficulty in the world which they cannot overcome.'

'A Communist should have largeness of mind and he should be staunch and active, looking upon the interests of the revolution as his very life and subordinating his personal interests to those of the revolution; always and everywhere he should adhere to principle and wage a tireless struggle against all incorrect ideas and actions, so as to consolidate the collective life of the Party and strengthen the ties between the Party and the masses; he should be more concerned about the Party and the masses than about any individual, and more concerned about others than about himself. Only thus can he be considered a Communist.'

Quotations from Chairman Mao Tse-tung (London and New York: Bantam Books, 1967), pp. 1, 3, 6, 33, 55, 65, 112 and 153.

DOCUMENT 10   THE 16-POINT DIRECTIVE ON THE CULTURAL REVOLUTION

This document, officially adopted on 8 August 1966, became the basis for the Great Proletarian Cultural Revolution. The following extracts call on the Chinese people to wage a new kind of revolution, to reform totally all aspects of Chinese life.

1. *A New Stage in the Socialist Revolution.* The Great Proletarian Cultural Revolution now unfolding is a great revolution that touches people to their very souls and constitutes a new stage in the development of the socialist revolution in our country, a stage which is both broader and deeper. ...

Although the bourgeoisie has been overthrown, it is still trying to use the old ideas, culture, customs and habits of the exploiting classes to corrupt the masses, capture their minds and endeavor to stage a comeback. The proletariat must do the exact opposite: it must meet head-on every challenge of the bourgeoisie in the ideological field and use the new ideas, culture, customs and habits of the proletariat to change the mental outlook of the whole of society. At present, our objective is to struggle against and overthrow those persons in power taking the capitalist road, to criticize and repudiate the bourgeois reactionary academic 'authorities' and the ideology of the bourgeoisie and all other exploiting classes and to transform education, literature, and art and all other parts of the super-structure not in correspondence with the socialist economic base, so as to facilitate the consolidation and development of the socialist system.

2. *The Main Current and the Twists and Turns.* Since the Cultural Revolution is a revolution, it inevitably meets with resistance. This resistance comes chiefly from those persons in power taking the capitalist road who have wormed their way into the Party. It also comes from the force of habits from the old society. At present, this resistance is still fairly strong and stubborn. But after all, the Great Proletarian Cultural Revolution is an irresistible general trend. There is abundant evidence that such resistance will be quickly broken down once the masses become fully aroused. ...

4. *Let the Masses Educate Themselves in the Movement.* ... Trust the masses, rely on them and respect their initiative. Cast out fear. Don't be

afraid of disturbances. Chairman Mao has often told us that revolution cannot be so very refined, so gentle, so temperate, kind, courteous, restrained and magnanimous. Let the masses educate themselves in this great revolutionary movement and learn to distinguish between right and wrong and between correct and incorrect ways of doing things. ...

Make the fullest use of big-character posters and great debates to argue matters out, so that the masses can clarify the correct views, criticize the wrong views and expose all ghosts and monsters. In this way, the masses will be able to raise their political consciousness in the course of the struggle, enhance their abilities and talents, distinguish right from wrong and draw a clear line between ourselves and the enemy.

David Milton, Nancy Milton, and Franz Schurmann, *The China Reader: People's China*
(New York: Random House, 1974), pp. 272–83.

DOCUMENT 11   ACCOUNTS OF THE CULTURAL REVOLUTION

Yue Daiyun, a university professor, was witness to much of the violence that marked the early stages of the Cultural Revolution (CR). The following selection, from her account of events in August 1966, is part of China's 'scar literature' – books that detail individual experiences during the CR.

Violence, brutality, tragedy became commonplace at Beida[1] that August. Every day and night small groups of four or five would be picked up to be criticized in their departments and then paraded through the campus to 'accept struggle from the masses'. The targets of these 'mass ground struggle sessions' would always be forced to balance on one of the high, narrow dining hall benches and told to answer questions. If the answers were considered unsatisfactory, the person's head would be pushed down or he would be instructed to bend low or he would be held in the agonizing jet plane position, continually begging the people's pardon for his past offenses. Because I lived in the area of the student dormitories, I would see several groups of some twenty or thirty people conducting these struggle sessions every night when I went out after supper to read the latest wall posters by lamplight. Usually the abuse would last for about an hour, then the victim would be allowed to return home.

One evening I had gone out to read the new posters when I came upon a group of students surrounding a teacher from the math department, a woman who had graduated in the same class as I, standing on one of those benches, her hair disheveled and a big placard across her chest announcing that she was an active counter-revolutionary. She had once remarked that the Cultural Revolution was wrong, I learned, and when her comment was reported, she was taken into custody and held somewhere on campus, perhaps in a classroom building. Suddenly out of the crowd I heard her husband's voice declaring with icy piety that he could never live with her again, that their relationship was finished, that she was no longer the mother of their three children. Following his denunciation, the Red Guards commanded her again to admit her guilt. Provoked by her silence, they shoved her head down very low, knocking out all of her hairpins and causing her hair to fall forward and cover her face. I had seen such scenes of humiliation and abuse many times by then, but never had I heard such a heartless repudiation by a husband.

Witnessing such daily cruelty had a numbing effect. One evening when I returned home after doing my labor, I saw my neighbor's cook and lifetime friend sitting on the threshold weeping. The neighbor, the chairman of the physics department and an especially kind old man who had never married, had returned home that day after a particularly harsh struggle session. The cook had discovered him with a scarf tied around his neck, hanging from the ceiling. Hearing the news of this latest tragedy, I recalled how after I had been condemned as a rightist, when I was shunned by everyone, this professor would always smile warmly at me and say hello when he worked in his courtyard, and how he had tried to save his favorite student from being exiled to the countryside. I thought bitterly that it was better for him to be dead, as he was now over seventy and couldn't bear such harsh treatment. His body was quickly taken away to be cremated, and no one mentioned him again.

---

[1] 'Beida' is a contraction for 'Beijing Daxue' or Beijing University.

Yue Daiyun and Carolyn Wakeman, *To the Storm: The Odyssey of a Revolutionary Chinese Woman* (Berkeley, CA: University of California Press, 1985) pp. 180–2.

DOCUMENT 12   THE 'TEN LOST YEARS' OF THE CULTURAL REVOLUTION

Following the Cultural Revolution, many Chinese felt that ten years of their lives had been wasted. The following selection is from a satirical short story, 'Ten Years Deducted', written by Shen Rong, a woman writer. Her collection of stories, At Middle Age, *was a Chinese bestseller in the late 1970s and included this story.*

Word wafted like a spring breeze through the whole office building. 'They say a directive will be coming down, deducting ten years from everybody's age!'

'Wishful thinking,' said a sceptic.

'Believe it or not,' was the indignant retort. 'The Chinese Age Research

Association after two years' investigation and three months' discussion has drafted a proposal for the higher-ups. It's going to be ratified and issued any day now.'

The sceptic remained dubious.

'Really? If so, that's the best news I ever heard!'

His informant explained:

'The age researchers agreed that the ten years of the "cultural revolution" wasted ten years of everyone's precious time. This ten years debit should be canceled out...'

'Deduct ten years and instead of sixty-one I'll be fifty-one – splendid!'

'And I'll be forty-eight, not fifty-eight – fine!'

'This is wonderful news!'

'Brilliant, great!'

The gentle spring breeze swelled up into a whirlwind engulfing everyone.

'Have you heard? Ten years deducted!'

'Ten years off, no doubt about it.'

'Minus ten years!'

All dashed around to spread the news.

An hour before it was time to leave the whole building was deserted. ...

'Little Lin, there's a dance tomorrow at the Workers' Cultural Palace. Here's a ticket for you.' Big sister Li of the trade union beckoned to Lin Sufen.

Ignoring her, Sufen quickened her step and hurried out of the bureau.

Take off ten years and she was only nineteen. No one could call her an old maid any more. The trade union needn't worry about a slip of a girl. She didn't need help from the matchmakers' office either. Didn't need to attend dances organized to bring young people together. All that was done with!

Unmarried at twenty-nine she found it hard to bear the pitying, derisive, vigilant or suspicious glances that everyone cast at her. She was pitied for being single, all alone; scoffed at for missing the bus by being too choosey; guarded against as hyper-sensitive and easily hurt; suspected of being hysterical and warped. One noon when she went to the boiler room to poach herself two eggs in a bowl of instant noodles, she heard someone behind her comment:

'Knows how to cosset herself.'

'Neurotic.'

She swallowed back tears. If a girl of twenty-nine poached herself two eggs instead of having lunch in the canteen, did that make her neurotic? What theory of psychology was that?

Even her best friends kept urging her to find a man to share her life. As if to be single at twenty-nine were a crime, making her a target of public criticism, a natural object of gossip. The endless idle talk had destroyed her peace of mind. Was there nothing more important in the world, no more urgent business than finding yourself a husband? How wretched, hateful, maddening, and ridiculous!

Now she had been liberated. I'm a girl of nineteen, so all of you shut up! She looked up at the clear blue sky flecked with small white clouds like handkerchiefs to gag those officious gossips. Wonderful! Throwing out her chest, glancing neither to right or left, she hurried with a light step to the bicycle shed, found her 'Pigeon' bicycle and flew off like a pigeon herself through the main gate.

It was the rush hour. The crowded streets were lined with state stores, collectively run or private shops. Pop music sounded on all sides. 'I love you...' 'You don't love me...' 'I can't live without you...' 'You've no place in your heart for me...' To hell with that rubbish!

Love was no longer old stock to be sold off fast. At nineteen she had plenty of time, plenty of chances. She must give top priority now to studying and improving herself. Real knowledge and ability could benefit society and create happiness for the people, thereby earning her respect, enriching her life and making it more significant. Then love would naturally seek her out and of course she wouldn't refuse it. But it should be a quiet, deep, half-hidden love.

She must get into college. Nineteen was just the age to go to college. There was no time to be wasted. ...

Shen Rong, *At Middle Age* (Beijing: Chinese Literature Press, 1987), pp. 343–64.

DOCUMENT 13   FANG LIZHI ON MODERNIZATION AND DEMOCRACY IN CHINA

The following paragraphs are taken from Dr Fang Lizhi's best-known speech, delivered in Shanghai on 18 November 1986.

Our goal at present is the thorough modernization of China. We all have a compelling sense of the need for modernization. There is a widespread demand for change among people in all walks of life; and very few find any reason for complacency. None feel this more strongly than those of us in science and academia. Modernization has been our national theme since the Gang of Four were overthrown ten years ago, but we are just beginning to understand what it really means. In the beginning we were mainly aware of the grave shortcomings in our production of goods, our economy, our science and technology, and that modernization was required in these areas. But now we understand our situation much better. We realize that grave shortcomings exist not only in our 'material civilization' but also in our 'spiritual civilization' – our culture, our ethical standards, our political institutions – and that these also require modernization.

Why is China so backward? To answer this question, we need to take a clear look at history. China has been undergoing revolutions for a century, but we are still very backward. This is all the more true since Liberation, these decades of the socialist revolution that we all know firsthand as students and workers. Speaking quite dispassionately, I have to judge this era a failure. This is not my opinion only, by any means; many of our leaders are also admitting as much, saying that socialism is in trouble everywhere. Since the end of World War II, socialist countries have by and large not been successful. There is no getting around this. As far as I'm concerned, the last thirty-odd years in China have been a failure in virtually every aspect of economic and political life.

We need to take a careful look at why socialism has failed. Socialist ideals are admirable. But we have to ask two questions about the way they have been put into practice: Are the things done in the name of socialism actually socialist? And, do they make any sense? We have to take a fresh look at these questions and the first step in that process is to free our minds from the narrow confines of orthodox Marxism.

We've talked about the need for modernization and reform, so now let's consider democracy. Our understanding of the concept of democracy is so inadequate that we can barely even discuss it. With our thinking so hobbled by old dogmas, it is no wonder we don't achieve democracy in practice. Not long ago it was constantly being said that calling for democracy was equivalent to requesting that things be 'loosened up'. In fact the word 'democracy' is quite clear, and it is poles apart in meaning from 'loosening up'. If you want to understand democracy, look at how people understand it in the developed countries, and compare that to how people understand it here, and then decide for yourself what's right and what's wrong.

Democracy is based on recognizing the rights of every single individual. Naturally, not everyone wants the same thing, and therefore the desires of different individuals have to be mediated through a democratic process, to form a society, a nation, a collectivity. But it is only on the foundation of recognizing the humanity and rights of each person that we can build democracy. However, when we talk about 'extending democracy' here, it refers to your superiors 'extending democracy' for you. This is a mistaken concept. This is not democracy.

In democratic countries, democracy begins with the individual. *I* am the master, and the government is responsible to *me*. Citizens of democracies believe that the people maintain the government, paying taxes in return for services – running schools and hospitals, administering the city, providing for the public welfare. ... A government depends on the taxpayers for support and therefore *has to be* responsible to its citizens. This is what people think in a democratic society. But here in China, we think the opposite way. If the government does something commendable, people say, 'Oh, isn't the government great for providing us with public transportation.' But this is really something it *ought* to be doing in exchange for our tax money. ... You have to be clear about who is supporting whom economically, because setting this straight leads to the kind of thinking that democracy requires. Yet China is so feudalistic that we always expect superiors to give orders and inferiors to follow them. What our 'spiritual civilization' lacks above all other things is the spirit of democracy. If you want reform – and there are more reforms needed in our political institutions than I have time to talk about – the most crucial thing of all is to have a democratic mentality and a democratic spirit.

Fang Lizhi, *Bringing Down the Great Wall: Writings on Science, Culture, and Democracy in China*. Translated by James H. Williams (New York: W.W. Norton & Co., 1990), pp. 157–88.

DOCUMENT 14   CCP STATEMENT ON THE EVENTS OF 4 JUNE 1989

The following was broadcast by China's official Xinhua News Agency in Chinese on 9 June 1989, to provide the public with the 'facts' of the Tiananmen Square 'rebellion'.

A shocking counter-revolutionary rebellion took place in the capital of Beijing on the 3rd and 4th of June following more than a month of turmoil. Owing to the heroic struggle put up by the martial law enforcement officers and men of the People's Liberation Army [PLA], the Armed Police Force, and public security cadres and police, as well as the cooperation and support of large numbers of people, initial victory has been won in suppressing the rebellion. However, this counter-revolutionary rebellion has not yet been put down completely. A handful of rioters are still hatching plots, spreading rumors to confuse and poison people's minds, and launching counterattacks. They are firing in the dark with firearms and ammunition they have seized; they are burning motor vehicles, smashing police boxes, and storming stores and public places in an attempt to put up a last-ditch struggle. Many rumors are now being spread in society, and many members of the masses have yet to understand the truth of the facts; they still have some problems to solve ideologically and emotionally. Therefore, it is necessary to clearly tell the masses about the truth of this counter-revolutionary rebellion to enable them to understand the causes and effects of the rebellion and the necessity and urgency of suppressing it. In this way, the masses will throw themselves into the struggle and contribute to stabilizing the situation in the capital. ...

In the early morning hours of June 4, a group of rioters at a junction on Dongdan Road attacked fighters with bottles, bricks, and bicycles. The faces of the fighters were covered with blood. At Fuxing Gate a vehicle was intercepted. All 12 fighters, including the chief of the administrative department of a military unit, members of the department, and cooks, were dragged from the vehicle and forcefully searched. After that, they were beaten soundly. Many of them were seriously wounded. At Liubukou four fighters were surrounded and beaten. Some of them died on the spot. ... At Huguo Temple after a military vehicle was intercepted, its fighters were dragged down, beaten soundly, and held hostage. A number of submachine guns were taken. ...

After dawn, the beating and killing of PLA fighters reached a degree that made one's blood boil. While an armed police detachment was carrying eight wounded fighters to a nearby hospital, it was intercepted by a group of rioters. After killing one of the fighters on the spot, the rioters threatened to kill the other seven. ...

Here are the facts. After the martial law enforcement units entered the square, the Beijing Municipal People's Government and the command of the martial law enforcement units issued an emergency notice at 0130 [1630 GMT]: 'A serious counter-revolutionary rebellion has occurred in the capital this evening. Rioters have savagely attacked PLA commanders and fighters, seized arms and munition, burned military vehicles, set up road barricades, and kidnapped PLA commanders and fighters in a vain attempt to subvert the People's Republic of China and overthrow the socialist system. The PLA has exercised utmost restraint for the past several days. Now it must resolutely strike back at the counter-revolutionary rebellion. Citizens in the capital must abide by the provisions of the martial law order and closely cooperate with the PLA in resolutely defending the constitution, the great socialist motherland, and the capital. Those who refuse to listen to our advice will have to be entirely responsible for the consequences because it will be impossible to ensure safety.'

At 0430, the notice of the Martial Law Command was broadcast in the square: 'Evacuation from the square will begin now. We agree to the students' appeal on evacuating from the square.'

Upon hearing the notice, the several thousand young students remaining in the square immediately assembled and deployed pickets who linked their hands. At around 0500, holding their banners, they began to move out of the square in an orderly way. The martial law troops left a wide opening in the southern entrance of the eastern side of the square, thereby ensuring the swift, smooth, and safe withdrawal of the students. At this time, there were still a small number of students who persistently refused to leave. In accordance with the demands of the 'circular', soldiers of the Armed Police Force forced them to leave the square. The square evacuation task was completely carried out by 0530. During the entire course of evacuation, which took less than 30 minutes, not a single one of the sit-in students in the square, including those who were forced to leave the square at the end, died. The claim that 'blood has formed a stream in Tiananmen' is sheer nonsense.

Xinhua New Agency, translated in Foreign Broadcast Information Service (FBIS-CHI-89-111) 12 June 1989, pp. 62–6.

DOCUMENT 15   PRIVATIZATION OF STATE-OWNED ENTERPRISES

This article highlights a woman entrepreneur who took over a failing government-owned factory and turned it around in 1999.

'I argued with myself for two months,' recalls Hu Ying. 'One moment I'd think, go ahead and buy it. The next moment I'd think, forget it. This is too dangerous.'

Finally, in November 1997, Hu, a 40-year-old former local government official, took the plunge. She put down 1.2 million renminbi (US$145,100) to buy a 51% stake in the troubled state-owned leather factory the government had assigned her to run 18 months earlier.

With that move, Hu became part of the mass privatization of small and medium-sized state-owned companies across China. To the consternation of China's vocal but marginalized conservative Marxists, China's leaders say they are committed to keeping a controlling interest only in large state enterprises and in companies in select industries, such as public utilities and communications.

Right in the forefront of the privatization movement is Hu's home town of Leshan, a city of 3.4 million people located three hours drive southwest of Chengdu, in western China. Over the past two years, Leshan has sold over 80% of its more than 400 small state manufacturing enterprises – those with net assets of 20 million renminbi or less. It wanted to sell them all, but some were in such bad shape that no one would have them. ...

Today, the renamed Leshan Lucky Dove Leather Co. is a busy place. It exported 300,000 garments in 1998, earning nearly US$1 million. Hu credits a strong emphasis on quality control, and the flexibility in setting salaries, assigning tasks and hiring workers that she gained when the company ceased to be state-owned.

Under state ownership, for example, the government Labour Bureau set pay scales. Employees who worked hard earned the same as those who didn't. Hu says she changed work attitudes by telling employees: 'If you don't work, we won't pay you.' She says 77 employees quit, and she has signed fixed-term contracts with the rest. ...

Like Leshan Mayor Liu, Hu believes Lucky Dove's privatization has been good for the state. 'If the enterprise develops and pays taxes, the government can still get a high return,' she says. In addition, Lucky Dove is now paying the bank interest on its outstanding debts.

Susan V. Lawrence, 'Selling the Burden', *Far Eastern Economic Review*, 18 February 1999, pp. 15–16.

DOCUMENT 16 UNDERGROUND CHRISTIAN CHURCHES

Only those religious groups which register with the Chinese government are allowed to practice their religions. Those who refuse to comply are subject to arrest, as recounted in the following news release.

Beijing, Sept. 1, 2000. China has arrested a priest, 20 nuns and three others from an underground Catholic church in southern Fujian province, in an ongoing crackdown on religious groups refusing to adhere to Communist Party ideology, a rights group said Friday. Police arrested Father Liu Shozhang Wednesday and beat him severely, causing him to vomit blood, the US-based Cardinal Kung Foundation said in a statement sent to Beijing.

Also arrested were 20 nuns, one seminarian and two lay persons who belong to the same church, an underground Roman Catholic Church in Gongtou Village in Fujian's capital, Fuzhou, the Foundation said.

A police official on Friday told AFP [Agence France Presse] the group was arrested when police found them using a mushroom processing factory for church services. He said police confiscated religious articles from the group and turned them over to county police. County police declined to comment.

Two of the nuns were released Thursday after a group of parishioners paid a large sum of money to the police bureau, the Foundation said. They were ordered not to leave their house unless they received permission from the police.

The remaining 22 people are still detained and their whereabouts are unknown, the Foundation said.

The arrests come less than two weeks after another priest was detained in Fujian. Father Gao Yihua was detained on August 19 and released on August 29, the Foundation said. An archbishop in Fuzhou, Yang Shudao, who was arrested on February 10 and released shortly afterwards, remains under heavy surveillance with several guards staying in his house 24 hours a day, the Foundation said.

The Foundation said China has recently begun a new crackdown to force members of the underground Roman Catholic Church to register with the Chinese government and join the Patriotic Association, which was set up to monitor and force religious groups to conform to Communist Party ideology. Two Catholic churches co-exist in China. The official one pledging allegiance to the Communist Party and rejecting the authority of the pope has between four and five million members, according to Beijing. The other clandestine church is loyal to the pope and is said to count around 10 million followers. ...

Other religious groups have also come under pressure in recent weeks. Fifty underground Protestants have been detained in three provinces in the past month and another 130 Protestants from an underground church in central Henan province were detained last week.

'China Arrests 24 Catholics from Underground Church', 1 September 2000,

Agence France Presse.

DOCUMENT 17   **ATHEISM IN CHINA**

Although religious practice is allowed in China, the government makes it clear that Party members are required to follow the official ideology that includes atheism. For minority cadres, this proved particularly difficult, as religion was seen as a part of their cultural identities. In this article from northwest China, Party members are reminded of their responsibility to serve as models for the area's largely Muslim population.

Urumqi *Xinjiang Ribao* [The Xinjiang Daily] 9 April 1997 – Considering the religious issue for party members as an important part of a party member's education, the Turpan prefectural party committee has carried out in-depth atheist education throughout the prefecture and brought about encouraging changes in the ideological and spiritual outlook of the broad masses of party members.

Turpan prefecture is an area where many ethnic groups, mostly Islamic, are concentrated. The number of believers is great and the religious belief is strong. Under the strong influence of religious belief, some party members' ideology has been corroded and they have begun to believe in religion or participate in religious activities in different degrees. Before the 4th plenary session of the 14th party central committee, 25% of the more than 18,000 party members in Turpan Prefecture were religious believers. In some villages, the percentage was over 40. A small number of party members even withdrew from the party because of their religious belief. Party members engaging in religious activities not only impair the image and authority of the party among the people and weaken the fighting force of party organizations but also encourage religious fanaticism and affect social stability. Through investigations and fact-finding, the Turpan prefectural party committee acquired a better understanding of the seriousness of the issue of religious party members and of the necessity and urgency of carrying out atheistic education. The prefectural party committee called a special meeting to include the education in atheism in the prefecture's general plan for education of party members and the objective control of party improvement, making this education a regular part of ideological and political work.

Atheistic education is based on a positive approach. They have conscientiously organized the broad masses of party members to study the basic concepts of Marxist dialectical materialism, Deng Xiaoping's theory of building Chinese-style socialism, the party's constitution, the party's religious policy, and scientific know-how. In accordance with the contents of education, the prefecture compiled, printed, and circulated 81,600 volumes (sets) of teaching materials about atheism to guarantee the learning needs of party members. ...

... The prefecture has established a party member objective control system at different levels, constantly checked on the ideological condition of party members, and provided immediate education and assistance when any party member is found to have engaged in religious activities. Grassroots democratic evaluations at all levels have carried out annual democratic evaluation of party members which consider the religious status of a party member as an important element, thus subjecting party members to supervision inside and outside the party. Those party members who firmly believe in religion and who refuse to change their ways after education should be given a certain time period to make corrections, be persuaded to withdraw from the party, or dismissed from the party according to the seriousness of their case. In recent years, 98 religious party members have been dealt with. Of them, six have been dismissed from the party, 62 persuaded to withdraw from the party, and four have lost political and living privileges.

Quan Deyi, 'Education in Atheism for Xinjiang Party Members', in *Xinjiang Ribao* [*Xinjiang Daily*] 9 April 1997.

DOCUMENT 18   MEASURES OF MODERNIZATION

The following collection of facts and figures on modern China indicates the improving standard of living enjoyed under the ongoing economic reforms.

Gross national product per capita, 1996, in US$	
China	750
Germany	28,870
India	380
Japan	40,940
Mexico	3,670
Russia	2,410
South Africa	3,520
USA	28,020

Infant mortality: number of deaths per 1,000 live births, 1996

China	33
Germany	5
India	65
Japan	4
Mexico	32
Russia	17
South Africa	49
USA	7

Military funding as a percentage of GNP, 1995

China	2.3
Germany	1.9
India	2.4
Japan	1.0
Mexico	1.0
Russia	11.4
South Africa	2.2
USA	3.8

Water pollution: emissions of organic pollutants, million lb/day

China	11.7
Germany	2.3
India	3.2
Japan	3.4
Mexico	0.4
Russia	n.a.
South Africa	0.6
USA	5.5

Number of privately-owned cars and buses in China

1990	240,700
1996	1,400,000

Number of telephones in China

1995	6.3 million
1996	70.5 million [only 15.1 million of the phones were in rural areas]

DOCUMENT 19   US–CHINA RELATIONS

Despite the ups and downs of US–China relations at the turn of the twenty-first century, some observers saw commerce as the key element bringing the two countries closer, suggesting that economic interdependence will override other issues.

It may have escaped most people's notice, but April was a busy month for China–United States business ties. United Airlines and United Parcel Service both opened new direct flights to China. A slew of new investments were announced – ranging from Ford Motor's 49 million bet on a Chongqing compact-car venture to Wisconsin-based CNH Global's $45 million plunge into a tractor factory in Shanghai. Meanwhile, the mayor of Denver was marching around China with 50 executives in tow in an effort to promote bilateral trade. All this while the two countries were engaged in their most serious military confrontation since ties were established in 1979.

The collision between an American spy plane and a Chinese fighter off the south China coast on April 1 set off a war of words that recalled the darkest days of the Cold War. Bilateral ties were also strained over Taiwan. US President George W. Bush promised new submarines, destroyers, and aircraft to Taiwan on April 24, and pledged the next day to do 'whatever it took' to help the island defend itself against a mainland invasion. Washington also gave a transit visa to former Taiwan President Lee Teng-hui. Beijing protested loudly.

But while diplomats on both sides managed to steal the media limelight from businessmen for most of the month, it is the businessmen who are increasingly driving the relationship between the US and China. As a result, the impact of the diplomatic confrontation is likely to remain muted.

As the US economy slips close to recession and Western markets flounder, China is offering one of the few big markets and investment opportunities for US companies. At the same time, China's leaders are desperate to maintain rapid growth – targeted at 8% this year – in order to stave off social unrest and undertake much-needed reforms. ...

Consider how business ties between the two nations have grown since 1995, the last time bilateral military tensions peaked following Chinese missile tests off Taiwan. From 1995 to last year, US annual investment in China rose 50% to $4.5 billion, making it the largest source of foreign investment in the mainland after Hong Kong. Over the same period, bilateral trade doubled to $116 billion. The US now buys a third of China's exports, many of them made by US companies in China. Entry to the World Trade Organization is expected to make China a bigger buyer, too.

Bruce Gilley and Murray Hiebert, 'Diplomacy of the Dollar', *Far Eastern Economic Review*, 10 May 2001, pp. 16–17.

DOCUMENT 20   CHINA AND TAIWAN

With the defeat of the Nationalist (Guomindang) Party on Taiwan in the 2000 presidential elections, power shifted into new hands. The new Vice President, Annette Lu, wrote about her views on Taiwan's relations with China in this article in the Harvard International Review.

The end of the Cold War has prompted both optimistic predictions of the sustainable peace and a more pessimistic view that a renewal of traditional rivalries between nation-states is likely. In any case, the long-standing Taiwan Strait issue remains a very real concern in the post-Cold War era. In 1995 and 1996, the People's Republic of China (PRC) launched a series of missile tests off Taiwan's shores in the hopes of dissuading Taiwanese voters from supporting pro-independence candidates in the 1996 presidential elections of the Republic of China (ROC). This year the PRC used an official white paper to warn the Taiwanese electorate against voting for the independence-oriented Democratic Progressive Party (DPP) candidates running for office in Taiwan's second direct popular election of the ROC president and vice president. The world watched closely as the PRC, an authoritarian power of growing economic and military might, threatened to use military force to influence Taiwan's democratic elections under the pretext of asserting the 'One China' principle. The voters in Taiwan were undaunted and demonstrated that they – and they alone – would decide who would be their next head of state.

Given the regularity of democratic elections in Taiwan, Beijing's predilection for interfering in the democratic process through provocative actions threatens to become a periodic threat to regional stability. Devising a suitable framework that places the cross-strait issue in a constructive context to overcome Beijing's self-imposed obstacles to progress and obviate the need for threats of military force is crucial for preserving stability in the Asia-Pacific region and the world. ...

Every community at one time or another experiences social division or political disputes. The manner in which these problems are resolved is a test of the collective wisdom of community members. The mechanism should be rational, just, and non-coercive if the resolution is to be long-lasting and constructive for the entire community. The same is true for cross-strait differences.

Every ruling entity in Chinese history so far has been created or toppled by military force. Mao Tsetung's statement that 'political power grows out of the barrel of a gun' is a vivid reminder of this mentality. To break this destructive cycle, the PRC leadership needs to adopt a new approach and embrace a few creative ideas – peaceful coexistence, peaceful competition, and a popular verdict. Let the PRC and Taiwan coexist peacefully and cooperate with each other. Eventually, the people of Taiwan will reach a verdict on whether or not they wish to integrate with the mainland. This might take a long time, but let history take its own course. If the Taiwanese of this generation do not believe that the time is ripe for Taiwan to integrate with the PRC, then Beijing should respect their will. If the next generation of Taiwanese prefer union with the PRC, then unification will take place peacefully and constructively.

To settle the thorny cross-strait issue, both Beijing and Taipei need to be 'creative, imaginative, and constructive.' Breaking out of the 'One China' cocoon might be necessary to set in motion an open negotiation process. The EU model may well provide an inspiring example not only for relations between the PRC and Taiwan, but also for relations among Asian states. I am sure that the ability to settle the cross-strait dispute peacefully will prove to be another index of the greatness of Chinese civilization. And if Asian countries can emulate the example of European integration, our region can look forward to a glorious and peaceful future.

Annette Lu, 'Shattering the "One China" Cocoon: A New Path for Taiwan and China',
Harvard International Review, Winter 2001.

DOCUMENT 21 CHINA AND CENTRAL ASIA

In the 1990s, China moved quickly to establish good relations with its new Central Asian neighbors who gained their independence with the collapse of the USSR. A major issue was the stability of Muslim Xinjiang where disaffected groups had staged demonstrations that led to violent confrontations with Chinese authorities. In 1997, new assurances were given to China by its immediate neighbors, as seen in the following selection.

Hong Kong AFP 18 June 1997 – Uighur exile groups seeking independence in northwestern China said on Wednesday that they can no longer count on help from neighboring Kyrgyzstan and Kazakhstan, following a visit there by the Chinese Defense Minister.

'We are not counting anymore on Kyrgyzstan and Kazakhstan to help us in the fight for the independence of Xinjiang, 'Mukhidin Mukhlissi, spokesman for the United Revolutionary Front, the separatist Uighur group based in Kazakhstan, told AFP.

The shift came as Chinese Defense Minister Chi Haotian visited Kyrgyzstan, following a similar trip to Kazakhstan. He was to return to Beijing on Friday.

Both ex-Soviet republics border China and are home to about 300,000 ethnic Uighurs, a Moslem people who form the majority in Xinjiang. Chi has won support for his aim of cracking down on Uighur nationalist exile groups.

A Kyrgyz Defense Ministry spokesman said this week that 'the positions of Kyrgyzstan and China against separatism and religious extremism are identical.'

Over the past few weeks, security services in Kazakhstan have stepped up surveillance of several Uighur separatist groups in the republic. 'We are disappointed by the Central Asian governments' statements during Chi Haotian's visit,' said Kakhrama Khodzhaberdiyev, head of the Association of Uighur people, which is legally registered in Kazakhstan. 'Only the United States can help us. We are going to New York and Washington in July to meet with the State Department officials,' one Uighur leader in the Kazakh capital Almaty said.

Xinjiang, which borders Kazakhstan, has been plagued by violence in recent years as ethnic Uighurs fight for independence from Beijing. Up to 100 people died after clashes on February 5–6 between Uighurs and Chinese in Xinjiang frontier town of Yining, according to witness reports.

China rarely admits to any violence in the region but Uighur nationalist groups there claim that 57,000 Uighurs have been arrested by the Chinese authorities in Xinjiang since April 1996.

Although Kazakhstan has said it opposes the Uighurs' separatist bid, it has also blamed China for human rights abuses in Beijing's dealings with the activists.

'Uighur Separatist Exiles See End to Central Asian Help', Agence France Presse report from
Hong Kong, 18 June 1997.

GLOSSARY

Agrarian Reform Law of 1950 Law authorizing the redistribution of land in China, as a result of which approximately half of the farm land in China was redistributed, mainly by confiscating the land holdings of wealthy families and allotting it to poorer families.

Agricultural Producers Cooperative Begun in 1955, these organizations called upon the peasant-farmers of China to pool all their resources and their land in order to increase production which was, in the CCP's view, impeded by the existence of small, individual plots of land. These in turn led to the formation of the communes in 1958.

Anti-Rightist Campaign A political campaign launched in the summer of 1957 to identify and remove from positions of power members of the CCP who were not adequately 'left' or pro-Communist in their thinking. Many Party stalwarts were sent for re-education in remote rural areas, despite years of dedicated service to the CCP cause.

Beijing Spring The period of April, May and early June of 1989 when student-led demonstrations in the capital city of Beijing appeared to be pushing the CCP toward greater democratization. The 'Spring' ended on 4 June 1989, with the PLA clearing Tiananmen Square by force and, in the process, killing an unknown number of people.

Big Character Posters See *Dazibao*.

Buddhism A universal, world religion based on the teachings of the historical Buddha of the sixth century BCE in the area of present-day Nepal. The basic tenets focus on the escape from pain and suffering which marks all human life and ending the cycle of repeated birth and death by following moral precepts and, ultimately, attaining a state of enlightenment.

Cadre A supporter of the Communist cause engaged in work on behalf of the movement. Cadre may also indicate a member of the Communist Party in China. The Chinese language equivalent is *ganbu*.

Capitalist roader Epithet used during the Cultural Revolution against those in positions of authority deviating from the Maoist line. Among those so accused in 1966 were Liu Shaoqi and Deng Xiaoping.

CCP Acronym for the Chinese Communist Party. Founded in July 1921 by a small group of intellectuals and students in Shanghai, the CCP grew slowly at first, but gained a large following during the Second World War, enabling it to defeat the Nationalist Party of Jiang Jieshi in 1949.

Central Committee of the Chinese Communist Party This elite group, which has varied in size from 100 to 300, includes all top leaders of the CCP and is the source of Party policy. Membership on the Central Committee is limited to the highest ranked members of the CCP.

Civil War   After the Second World War, efforts at mediation between the two leading parties in China failed, and from 1946 to 1949 China experienced a civil war which ended in CCP victory in 1949.

Comintern   The Communist International, founded in the USSR by Lenin to spread Communism throughout the world. A number of Comintern agents worked with the Communist and Nationalist Parties prior to the CCP victory in 1949.

Common Program   Adopted in 1949, this was the basis for China's government until it was replaced with the first constitution in 1954.

Commune   First formed in the summer of 1958 as a part of the Great Leap Forward, communes incorporated all peasant-farmers and workers into large work organizations intended to become self-sustaining economic and social units. Subdivided into brigades and teams, the communes were reduced in size in the early 1960s, but overall they proved inefficient and were dismantled in 1980–83.

Communism   A political philosophy which views the ideal society as one in which all property is held in common, class divisions disappear, and the state apparatus is no longer required; a utopian form of economic and social organization.

Confucius   A sixth-century BCE Chinese sage who stressed the need for harmony and balance in human affairs and whose teachings provided a moral, ethical code of behavior that endured for centuries in China.

Contract responsibility system   Adopted in the early 1980s as part of the reform era, this system allowed peasant-farmers to lease land and plant crops of their choice. Because of its success in increasing agricultural output, it replaced the commune system and remains the basis of the rural economy in China.

Conurbation   Densely populated urban area that includes a major city, its outlying suburbs, and small towns.

CPPCC   Acronym for the Chinese People's Political Consultative Conference which first convened in 1949 to pass the Common Program. The Program served as the legal basis for the new government and named Mao as China's head of state. The CPPCC continues to meet as an advisory body to the government of China.

CR   Acronym for the Cultural Revolution. The full name of this movement is the Great Proletarian Cultural Revolution. It was launched by Chairman Mao in 1966 and ended in 1976, the year that Mao died.

CUST   Acronym for China University of Science and Technology, a major technological university in the central Chinese province of Anhui.

Cultural Revolution   See *Great Proletarian Cultural Revolution*.

Dageda   Chinese term which, literally translated, means 'big brother dial'. It is the popular name for a cell phone.

Dalai Lama   The highest-ranking religious leader in Tibetan Buddhism. Having fled China in 1959, the fourteenth Dalai Lama established a Tibetan government in exile at his refuge in Dharmsala, India.

Danwei   Chinese term for work unit. Every worker belonged to a *danwei* which not only paid his or her salary, but also provided health care, housing, child care, and other services.

Daoism (or Taoism). An ancient school of thought in China derived from the observation of nature and the belief in dual forces of *yin* and *yang*, respectively represented by the moon and the sun, the negative and the positive, and the dark and the light. Daoism is one of the *san jiao*, or Three Teachings, of China; the other two are Buddhism and Confucianism.

Dazibao Chinese term for 'Big Character Poster'. A poster containing opinions and/or political slogans pasted on to walls in public places. The right of Chinese citizens to put up these posters was granted in the Chinese constitution of 1978, but the leadership revoked this and other forms of public expression in 1980 as part of efforts to curtail the democracy movement.

Democracy Wall Located in central Beijing on Changan Boulevard in 1978, this wall was covered with Big Character Posters in the early years of the democracy movement in China. After 1980, the wall was off limits to such posters, and although an alternative site was established for this particular form of public expression, its inconvenient location precluded its becoming an important site for democracy activists.

Dissident A person who actively opposes policies of their government, with which he or she strongly disagrees, and who does so despite personal risk.

DPP Acronym for Taiwan's Democratic Progressive Party which, in 2000, gained the Taiwan government presidency with the election of Chen Shuibian. President Chen is the first individual outside the Nationalist Party to hold this top office in Taiwan.

Encirclement and Annihilation Campaigns Five campaigns undertaken between 1931 and 1934 by the Nationalist Party under Jiang Jieshi (Chiang Kai-shek) intended to destroy the CCP. Only the last, conducted with German military advice, was able to dislodge the CCP which began its Long March in October 1934 to escape the Nationalist campaigns.

Fabi Chinese term for 'legal currency'. The term was replaced with *renminbi*, or people's currency, when the CCP came to power in 1949.

Falungong Also known as *Falun Dafa*, variously translated as the Law of the Wheel or Buddhist Law. A late twentieth-century spiritual movement based on the ancient teaching of *qigong*, a system of breathing exercises and physical movements, and on a mixture of Buddhist and Daoist beliefs. Banned in 1999, followers continued to defy the government by the public practice of their rituals. Arrests and detentions appeared to increase, rather than lessen; the number of adherents, and the crack-down on their activities has drawn renewed international criticism of China's religious policies.

Feminization of agriculture The predominance of female labor in agricultural work which became low-paid and low-status labor. Young men sought better pay and status in town or city enterprises, leaving women to work the family's leased land during the reform era.

Fifth modernization Democracy. Students called for the addition of this fifth item to the official 'Four modernizations' of the Deng era, demanding that the government not only modernize industry and agriculture, but also the government itself.

571 Affair   Shorthand for a plot against Mao by his Minister of Defense, Lin Biao, in September 1971. Lin's attempt at assassination failed, and his commandeered Air Force jet was reportedly shot down over Mongolia. A full account of the incident has yet to be written.

Floating population   As part of the reform era, restrictions on travel and movement in China loosened, allowing many rural workers to 'float' or move in search of employment. An estimated 120 million people were part of this mobile group at the end of the twentieth century.

Four Big Rights   In the 1978 Chinese constitution, the Chinese people were given the rights of *daming, dafang, dabianlun,* and *dazibao,* which meant, respectively, the right to speak out freely, air views fully, hold great debates and write Big Character Posters. These were all revoked in 1980 as part of government efforts to curtail the emergent democracy movement.

'Four Olds'   Denounced during the Cultural Revolution, the four 'old' practices that the CR tried to eradicate were old habits, customs, culture and thought. As part of this onslaught on the past, young Red Guards destroyed temples, religious sites, books, and Western goods like pianos and clothing.

Four Pests Campaign   A 1950s' campaign of the CCP to eliminate common pests throughout China, including rats, mosquitoes, flies, and sparrows.

Ganbu   See *Cadre.*

Gang of Four   Consisting of Chairman Mao's wife, Jiang Qing, and her three key supporters in the Cultural Revolution, this 'gang' was blamed for the excesses of the CR. In a show trial, Jiang Qing was sentenced to death for her actions; the sentence was commuted to life in prison.

GDP   Acronym for Gross Domestic Product. A figure produced by deducting the value of income earned on investments made by a country's citizens abroad from a country's total GNP; usually based on annual figures.

Geomancy   A form of divination which sought to improve future prospects or fortune by placing buildings or tombs in places considered to be auspicious; in Daoism, *feng shui,* which translates literally as wind-water, is a form of geomancy.

GMD   Acronym for Guomindang (also romanized as Kuomintang and abbreviated as KMT) and the same as the Nationalist Party. Originally founded by Dr Sun Zhongshan, the Party was dominated in the 1930s by Jiang Jishi and, following the Civil War, its leaders retreated to Taiwan where it remains an important political force.

GNP   Acronym for Gross National Product. The total value of a nation's annual output of goods and services.

Great Leap Forward   An economic movement launched by Mao in 1958 to make China the equal of Britain in 15 years. It led to widespread famine and the deaths of millions. As part of the Great Leap, the communes became the basic unit of socialist production and remained as such until the system was dismantled in the early 1980s.

Great Proletarian Cultural Revolution   A political movement launched by Chairman Mao Zedong in 1966 which became a violent assault on those considered disloyal to Mao and the Communist movement. Although the most extreme phase ended in 1969, the aftermath continued to affect the lives of millions until Mao's death in 1976. See also *Red Guards*.

Guomindang See *GMD*.

Han dynasty From 206 BCE to 220 CE, this important dynasty laid the foundations for the imperial Chinese state. Because of its importance, the name 'Han' is also an ethnonym used to distinguish 'Han' Chinese from ethnic minorities such as the Tibetans or Mongolians in China.

Hong Kong As a result of the treaty settlements after the Opium War of 1839–42, Hong Kong island, off the south China coast, was ceded in perpetuity to Britain. The original town on the island was called Victoria, in honor of Queen Victoria, but as the population increased and additional land was leased from China, the whole enclave came to be known as Hong Kong. Returned to China in 1997, the area is now a special administrative region of China.

Hui Chinese who follow Islam. Some Hui people trace their roots to the arrival of traders from the Arab world during the Tang dynasty (618–906 CE). This 'foreign' origin is cited as a reason for the Hui being classified as a national minority group, although their language and most of their cultural practices are the same as those of the Han Chinese population.

Iron rice bowl A term used to designate a permanent position, literally an unbreakable 'bowl' that guaranteed basic livelihood or 'rice'.

IUD Intrauterine device. A contraceptive device inserted by a physician to prevent pregnancy. This is the most commonly-used method of birth control in China.

Jiangxi Soviet Founded in 1931 in the border area of Jiangxi and Fujian, this was an area controlled by a 'Soviet' or governing council led by Mao Zedong. A number of 'Soviets' emerged in rural China after 1927 when the CCP moved underground, and the Jiangxi Soviet was the largest of these. It was abandoned in 1934 as a result of Nationalist attacks.

Korean War Conflict that began with the invasion of South Korea by North Korean Communist forces in June 1950 and ended with a UN-brokered truce in 1953, leaving Korea divided at the same border as when fighting began.

Kuomintang See *GMD*.

Landlord A man who held larger than average amounts of land and hired farm laborers to work it, or rented his land to others. In the 1950s, landlords and their families became the target of various campaigns and landlord status disadvantaged any individuals so labeled for over three decades.

'Little Red Book' Officially entitled *The Quotations of Chairman Mao*, this pocket-sized book, usually with bright red plastic covers, was carried by members of the Chinese military and by the young members of the Red Guards in the 1960s; after Mao's death in 1976, the books disappeared, re-emerging in the 1990s as tourist souvenirs.

Long March The journey of the CCP in retreat from the Jiangxi Soviet base after repeated attacks by the GMD, from October 1934 to December 1935. High attrition rates reduced the marchers from nearly 100,000 to 8,000 by the time they arrived at Yanan, in northern China.

Lop Nor   A lake, now a dry lake-bed, in eastern Xinjiang; the area is the site of China's nuclear testing program.

Lushan   A mountain retreat for CCP leaders and the site of the 1959 Lushan Conference at which Mao denounced his long-time colleague, Peng Dehuai, for criticizing the Great Leap Forward. Following the meeting, Mao stepped down as President of China, although he retained the title of Chairman of the CCP and head of the Chinese military.

Macao   A former Portuguese colony in south China, at the mouth of the Pearl River, near Hong Kong. Macao was returned to Chinese control in 1999 and became a special administrative region.

Manchuria   The ancestral lands of the Manchu people who established China's last dynasty, the Qing (1644–1912). In the 1930s, Japan occupied this area of northeastern China, and proclaimed it a new state, 'Manchukuo', under the last emperor of the Qing, Puyi, who served as a figure-head. The area reverted to Chinese control after 1945. After 1949, it was reorganized by the new Chinese government into the provinces of Heilongjiang, Jilin, and Liaoning.

Mao Zedong Thought   Also, Maoism. The political thought of Mao Zedong, including his interpretation of Marxism and Leninism, and derived from his various writings on socialism, capitalism, and communism.

Marriage Law of 1950   One of the first laws passed by the new CCP-led government of China, this made men and women legally equal, set minimum ages for marriage, and outlawed such practices as concubinage. Its most controversial clause granted women the right to sue for divorce.

Marriage Law of 1980   This revision of the original 1950 law raised the minimum age for marriage and also required all married couples to practice birth control, among other provisions.

May Fourth Movement   This political and intellectual movement began on 4 May 1919, as a protest against the Treaty of Versailles. As one of the allies in the First World War, China had hoped to benefit from the settlement, mainly in the form of treaty revisions with the European powers, but, instead, America and the European states granted Japan the former German concessions in China rather than returning them to Chinese control. The student-led protests of 4 May in major cities throughout China, led to a new intellectual awakening and the rise of Chinese nationalism. As a result of the protests, the Chinese government did not sign the treaty.

Mutual aid teams   These small groups of villagers were organized in the early 1950s to formalize the practice of sharing tools and draught animals among villagers in order to facilitate agricultural production. Based on the success of the teams, the CCP quickly moved to a higher stage of shared ownership and production which was much less popular.

National minority (shaoshu minzu)   Refers to ethnic groups with official recognition and legal status as minorities. Although some 400 groups requested this designation in the 1950s, only 56 groups are recognized as such, entitling them to participate in the regional autonomy system that was designed to ensure minorities a voice in local government.

National Party Congress   The body which chooses the top CCP leadership and the theoretical source of the CCP's legitimacy. The first Congress was held in 1921, at the time of the Party's formation, and Congresses have met irregularly ever since. The fourteenth NPC was held in 1992, with plenums, or additional sessions, held in succeeding years.

National People's Congress   Theoretically, the basis of legitimacy for the People's Republic of China, but in practice the Congress convenes irregularly for periods of one to two weeks, making it impossible for the body to have careful oversight of government policy or its implementation. The eighth Congress convened in March of 1993, with plenums, or additional sessions of the same Congress, held in succeeding years.

Nationalism   A political philosophy based on the idea that separate peoples have unique and distinctive traits; it often includes the notion that each people should have a separate and independent state.

Northern Expedition   A military campaign, from 1926 to 1928, undertaken by Jiang Jieshi (Chiang Kai-shek) to defeat the warlords and to unify China. Its success brought Jiang to the presidency of China, which he retained from 1928 onwards, except for brief, strategic 'retirements' from which he always re-emerged stronger politically.

'Old Feudal'   A term used to describe anyone still adhering to old ideas after the Communist revolution of 1949.

One-child Policy   The official policy limiting each couple to only one child. Rewards and punishments to enforce this policy were determined at the provincial level, and some punishments were very severe, drawing international criticism. In practice, couples could secure permission for a second child, particularly when the first child was female.

100 Flowers Campaign   Initiated in 1957 by Chairman Mao, this campaign called upon the people to offer criticism of policies and cadre behavior; the program was ended abruptly in early June 1957.

Opium Wars   The first war, primarily limited to coastal China in 1839–42, ended in the Treaty of Nanjing between Great Britain and China. The second war, 1856–58, involved France and Great Britain and ended in the Treaty of Tianjin. China's losses gave Western states greater privileges in China and began a period referred to as 'semi-colonialism' by the present government.

Organic Law of Villagers Committees   Passed in 1988, this law was intended to give local villages more say in the running of village governments and more autonomy for village officials. Through village-level elections, competition for local offices increased and gave villagers the opportunity to vote corrupt or incompetent officials out of office.

Patriarchy   Male dominance in society and in the family, reinforced in China by traditional Confucian values.

PLA   People's Liberation Army; the official name of China's armed forces.

PNTR   Permanent normal trade relations; granted to China by the United States in 2000, paving the way for China's entry into the WTO.

Politburo   Contraction for Political Bureau, members of which are chosen from the numerically larger Standing Committee of the Central Committee of the CCP. This group, almost exclusively male, is the most powerful group in China.

Qigong   Ancient form of breathing exercises mixed with physical movements to enhance health and prolong life.

Qin dynasty (221–208 BCE)   A relatively short dynasty which followed legalist principles in imposing a harsh rule of law over northern China. It provided a basis for the Han dynasty which followed it.

Qing   The last dynasty of China (1644–1912); founded by Manchus from northeastern China with assistance from their allies, the Mongols, and from Ming dynasty (1368–1644) generals who defected to the Manchus in 1644.

Qing Ming Festival   Also known as Tomb Sweeping Day, this ancient festival usually falls in April, and is marked by visits to local cemeteries where graves are cleaned and offerings are made to honor ancestors.

Qur'an (or Koran)   The sacred book of Islam, containing the teachings of the Prophet Mohammed, dating from the seventh century CE.

Rape of Nanjing   The assault on the civilian population of Nanjing by the Japanese army in December 1937. An estimated 100,000 non-combatants died, and countless women were raped in a three-week period.

Red Guards   Young people who participated in the Cultural Revolution, at the invitation and instigation of Chairman Mao, beginning in 1966. Initially drawn from the ranks of cadres' families, the movement expanded to include thousands of teenagers who viewed themselves as saving the revolution and purifying China of all counter-revolutionary tendencies. They were ordered to disband and return to their homes in 1969, after causing havoc throughout China.

Reform era   Dated from Deng Xiaoping's rise to power beginning in 1978 and continuing in 2002.

Regional autonomy system   Established to give minority groups a voice, 'autonomous' governments were formed at the lower levels first, culminating in the formation of five autonomous regions; each level included representatives of all nationalities living in the area. Although special powers were given to these units, in practice CCP domination ensured conformity with national government policy and allowed little or no deviation from Beijing-mandated policies.

Republic of China   The current government of the island of Taiwan, off the eastern coast of China, which maintains its claim as the legitimate government of all of China.

Responsibility system   See *Contract responsibility system*.

17-Point Agreement   The agreement signed in 1951 between representatives of the Tibetan leader, the Dalai Lama, and the new Chinese government. Both sides eventually repudiated the agreement which was in effect from 1951 until the spring of 1959.

SEZ (Special Economic Zones)   Instituted by Deng Xiaoping to jumpstart the Chinese economy in the reform era, these zones offered foreign investors generous terms in the form of tax relief and low costs. The most successful was Shenzhen, a rapidly growing city just across the border from Hong Kong.

Shanghai Communiqué   An agreement signed between the United States and China in 1972, declaring their mutual intention to open talks and explore the possibility of resuming official diplomatic relations.

Shenzhen   Former village just across the border from Hong Kong, Shenzhen was made an SEZ in 1980; in the next two decades, its population grew to 4 million, including a large, well-trained work force employed by international corporations manufacturing a wide range of goods.

Sino-Soviet split   This famous rift in Chinese–Soviet relations occurred in 1958 when Mao, angered at the Soviet leadership's attitude toward China, broke off relations. Soviet advisers then working in China were re-called, and relations between the two communist powers remained cold until the 1989 visit of Mikhail Gorbachev to China, in the midst of student demonstrations.

Siying   Chinese term for private enterprises.

Social Education Campaign   This political campaign to instill proper socialist values in the Chinese population was ordered by Chairman Mao in 1962, but the outcome fell short of his expectations, leading him to launch the Cultural Revolution in 1966.

Social gospel   The Christian Protestant movement to include education and medical services as part of their evangelical efforts in China prior to 1949.

'Speak Bitterness' Meetings   As part of the land redistribution process overseen by the CCP in 1950–53, villagers were encouraged to tell of their past abuse at the hands of local landlords, and these gatherings were thus an opportunity to speak of the 'bitter' past. The public denunciations drew peasants into the revolutionary process and often ended in the villagers sentencing the landlord to death.

State Environment Protection Administration   Created in 1998 to address increasing environmental pollution problems, the SEPA is to enforce laws and policies dealing with environmental protection.

Strike Hard Campaign   A police campaign intended to crack down on crime throughout China which began in the mid-1990s. The increased presence of policemen on the streets and in highly populated areas like markets and parks was noticeable, but complaints of less public crimes, such as bribery and the embezzling of public funds, continued throughout the campaign and still persist.

Taijiquan (T'ai Ch'i)   An ancient form of flowing physical exercise practiced by many Chinese for general health and well-being.

Taiwan   Island off the eastern coast of China, on which the Republic of China is based.

Takla Makan Desert   Located in the southern area of Xinjiang, the Takla Makan is one of the world's most arid places; it contains enormous natural gas and oil deposits, and is, therefore, marked for exploitation in the early twenty-first century.

Taoism   See *Daoism*.

Three Bitter Years   The years of 1959–61 are referred to as bitter years because of prolonged famine and food shortages throughout China, as a result of both man-made and natural disasters. During this time, an estimated 30 million Chinese people died.

Three Gorges Dam A major hydroelectric project which, when finished, will be the world's largest dam. Located in Sichuan province on the upper reaches of the Yangzi River, the resultant lake will flood acres of farmland as well as villlages, requiring the relocation of millions of people. The dam will supply electricity to western China where demand is enormous, although the cost of the dam in human and environmental terms has yet to be fully determined.

Three Obediences In traditional patriarchal China, a woman was taught to be obedient to her father during her childhood, to her husband when married, and to her son when she was widowed. These 'three obediences' meant that a woman would always be subservient to a male relative.

Tiananmen Square Massacre On 4 June 1989, the CCP leadership ordered the military to clear Tiananmen Square, an open area in the center of Beijing, where hundreds of students and their supporters continued their two-month-long demonstration. The term 'massacre' refers to the use of overwhelming military force against unarmed civilians, an unknown number of whom died.

Treaty of Alliance and Friendship This treaty between China and the USSR was signed in 1950; it provided for Soviet loans to China and the assignment of Soviet technicians to assist in China's modernization. The treaty was abrogated in 1958.

Treaty of Versailles This treaty was the settlement which followed the First World War, in which China played a minor role on the side of the European allies. Chinese expectations for generous treatment were dashed when former German concessions were granted to Japan rather than being returned to China. Following massive protests, China did not sign the treaty.

Uighurs A Turkic Muslim people, the majority of whom live in the Xinjiang-Uighur Autonomous Region in northwestern China. In 2000 the population was estimated at 9 million.

USSR Acronym for the Union of Soviet Socialist Republics. Founded in 1917 after the Bolshevik revolution ousted the tsar and took control of the former Russian empire, the USSR collapsed in 1991. Although the new Russian state lost many of its Central Asian republics, it retained control of Siberia and, therefore, continues to share a border with northeastern China.

Viet Nam War Initially a local conflict between the Communist forces of North Viet Nam and the American-backed Nguyen government of the South, the confrontation escalated with increased American involvement in the 1960s. The United States withdrew its troops in 1975, and in 1976 Viet Nam was united under Ho Chi-min's Communist Party.

Wan xi shao Chinese slogan translated as 'later, fewer, further between', which was used with the new family planning regulations to remind women that the government recommended having children later, having fewer in number, and spacing births by waiting four to five years between children.

Warlord Men who ruled areas of China through the exercise of military force. Between 1916 and 1928, the Central Government was unable to govern China effectively because warlords dominated large areas of China. Although some lost power during the Northern Expedition of 1926–28, in the north and west of China warlords continued to dominate provincial governments into the 1940s.

World Bank   Formed at the end of the Second World War to finance the rebuilding of war-torn states and the development of former colonies, the World Bank loans money to its member-states for projects all over the globe. China became a major borrower in the 1990s.

WTO   Acronym for the World Trade Organization The WTO is a global agency that sets trade regulations and requires all members to conform to global standards for trade and commerce.

Xiahai   Chinese term which literally translates as 'into the sea', but which came to mean leaving government positions to 'jump' into the new economy of the 1990s.

Xiamen   Chinese coastal city in Fujian province designated an SEZ as part of the reform era efforts to attract foreign investors to China.

Xinjiang-Uighur Autonomous Region   China's largest minority region, Xinjiang is home to Muslim peoples such as the Uighur, Kazak, Tajik, and Kyrgyz. Han migration into the region since 1949 has drastically changed the ethnic composition: from 5% of the population in 1949, Han now account for nearly 40%.

Yuan   A general Chinese term for money. Officially, the currency today is called *renminbi*, or the people's money.

Zhongnanhai   The private, guarded compound in Beijing which houses China's top leaders. It is located just to the west of the former imperial palace on Changan Boulevard.

Zunyi Conference   In January 1935, a meeting was held at Zunyi, a city in Guizhou province, by the leadership of the CCP resulting in the repudiation of Moscow-trained advisers and the decision to follow Mao, whose rise to the leadership of the CCP dates from this period.

Chen Shuibian (1950–)   Born in Taiwan, Chen led Taiwan's opposition party, the DPP, to victory in the 2000 presidential elections. Chen's government nonetheless had to contend with the Nationalist (GMD) Party which still controlled the legislature and other government positions. Relations with the PRC, just across the Taiwan Straits, remained the major challenge for Taiwan's new leader.

Chiang Ch'ing-kuo   See *Jiang Jingguo*.

Chiang Kai-shek   See *Jiang Jieshi*.

Dalai Lama   The highest-ranking religious figure within the Tibetan Buddhist religion. In addition to being a spiritual leader, most Tibetans regard the Dalai Lama as the rightful temporal leader of Tibet as well. The current Dalai Lama, the fourteenth man to hold this title, lives in India where he has headed a Tibetan government in exile since 1959.

Deng Xiaoping (1904–97)   Known as China's 'paramount' leader, Deng joined the communist movement in his teens and dedicated his life to the communist cause in China. A survivor of the Long March, he held a number of positions in the Party and the military, rising to Secretary-General of the Party before being vilified in the Cultural Revolution. By 1978, he had emerged as one of the top leaders once more and, with help from his key supporters, launched widespread reforms. His legacy of a more open China, stronger economy, and improved lives for millions of Chinese was marred by the Tiananmen Square Massacre of 1989 and growing corruption as the country shifted toward a market-driven economy.

Deng Yingzhao (1904–92)   Government official and activist, known for championing women's rights, particularly through the Chinese Women's Federation. The wife of Zhou Enlai, Deng held positions in the Party in her own right after 1976.

Fang Lizhi (1936–)   Astrophysicist at CUST, and currently a university professor in the United States. Fang was among China's leading scientists when he began to speak out against Chinese government policies in the 1980s. His outspoken criticism led to his being blamed for the student demonstrations of 1989, after which he was forced to leave China.

Hu Jintao (1943–)   Vice President and member of the Politburo. Hu rose through the Chinese Communist Youth League and held top party positions in Guizhou and, in 1988, in Tibet. In the 1990s, he was moved to Beijing where he served as President of the Central Party School and as a member of the Politburo. Hu ranked fifth in the Party hierarchy in 2001 and was widely considered a probable successor to China's presidency early in the twenty-first century.

Hu Yaobang (1915–89)   Former Secretary-General of the CCP in the 1980s. Hu was among the men chosen by Deng Xiaoping to inaugurate reforms in government and the CCP. However, in 1987 his support for student activists calling for greater democracy led to his dismissal from his post in 1987. His death, from natural causes, in April 1989 touched off the student demonstrations that marked the beginning of Beijing Spring.

Hua Guofeng (1921–)   Hua rose from relative obscurity to become Premier of China following the death of Mao in 1976. He was soon eased out of his top positions by Deng Xiaoping and replaced by Deng's own hand-picked men.

Jiang Jieshi (1887–1975)   President of China (1928–49) and on Taiwan from 1950 until his death in 1975. Jiang rose to power after the death of Dr Sun Zhongshan in 1925 through his military leadership of the Northern Expedition. Adamantly anti-Communist, Jiang pursued the CCP despite the growing Japanese threat. He belatedly began preparations to defend China in 1937 but the Japanese invasion forced him to retreat inland, to Chongqing in Sichuan province, where he and the Nationalists managed to hold on until the end of the Second World War. Despite considerable American aid after the war, Jiang lost to the CCP and retreated to Taiwan where he continued to lead the Nationalist Party until his death, one year before his nemesis, Mao Zedong.

Jiang Jingguo (1909–88)   Son of Jiang Jieshi by Jiang's first wife, the younger Jiang received his education in the USSR and married a Russian. In the 1940s, he held posts in the Nationalist-led government; after the move to Taiwan, he became head of the Nationalist secret police before assuming the presidency after his father's death in 1975. Like his father, he died in office, in 1988.

Jiang Qing (1914–91)   Third wife of Mao Zedong and major political figure in the Cultural Revolution. Jiang Qing began her career as a film actress; she married Mao in 1938. In 1966 she emerged from relative obscurity to take a major role in the CR. After Mao's death, she was widely blamed for the excesses of the CR and, following a show-trial in 1980–81, was sentenced to death; the sentence was later commuted to life imprisonment. She died in a prison hospital, reportedly by her own hand, in 1991.

Jiang Zemin (1926–)   President of China; Chairman of the CCP; head of the Chinese military. An engineer by training, Jiang's political career began in the 1950s, leading to his 1986 appointment as mayor of Shanghai. In 1989, Deng Xiaoping brought him to Beijing and supported his elevation to the top positions in the country. After Deng's death in 1997, Jiang's position as China's top leader was further affirmed with Jiang appointees moving into additional top posts in the government.

Li Denghui (Lee Teng-hui) (1929–)   President of China on Taiwan (1988–2000). American-educated Li was a native of Taiwan and thus the first native to hold the top political office on the island. He continued many of the policies he inherited from the Jiang family but also made some significant changes, including the lifting of restrictions on travel to China for Taiwan passport holders and recognizing the existence of the DPP which previously was denied the legal right to exist despite its large following.

Li Peng (1928–)   President, National People's Congress. Li was an adopted son of Zhou Enlai and Deng Yingzhao. Educated in the USSR as an engineer in the 1950s, Li held a number of positions in China's government and the CCP before being made Premier in 1988. Widely blamed for the Tiananmen Square Massacre, Li retained his position as Premier until 1998, after which he assumed the presidency of the National People's Congress.

Lin Biao (1907–71)   General in the PLA and Minister of Defense under Mao. Lin was a military hero of the Civil War and rose to become Defense Minister in the 1960s when he was also named as Mao's successor. A leader of the Cultural Revolution, he prepared the 'Little Red Book' of Mao's quotes used by thousands of PLA soldiers and Red Guards. Lin was accused of plotting against Mao in the '571 Affair' and the official CCP account asserts that he died in 1971 when his aeroplane was shot down over Mongolia as he fled China after the failed coup attempt.

Liu Binyan (1925–)   Dissident journalist. Liu worked as a journalist for the CCP newspaper, the *People's Daily*. Appalled by increasing corruption in the Party after 1980, he wrote a series of exposé articles for which he was finally expelled from the CCP. He chose to leave China and currently works as a human rights activist and writer in the United States.

Liu Shaoqi (1898–1969)   Former President of China. Liu was educated in the USSR and served the CCP mainly as a theoretician. Following the disaster of the Great Leap Forward, he became President of China and, through a series of cautious reforms, rebuilt the economy in the early 1960s.

Mao Zedong (1893–1976)   Chairman of the Chinese Communist Party and leader of China's Communist revolution. Born in rural Hunan province, Mao received a university degree and, upon moving to Beijing, was introduced to the ideas of Marx by founders of the CCP, Chen Duxiu and Li Dazhao. Mao led the Jiangxi Soviet government in 1931 and rose to prominence during the Long March when the CCP finally repudiated USSR leadership. He rebuilt the Party and its military units at Yanan during the Second World War, and led the CCP to victory in 1949. As Chairman of the CCP, Mao's accomplishments and failures have left a mixed assessment of his role after 1949, but he nonetheless is the single most important figure in the history of modern China.

Peng Dehuai (1898–1974)   PLA general. Peng gained prominence for his leadership during the Korean War, but his reputation was not adequate to protect him from Mao's denunciation of him in 1959, when Peng's negative appraisal of the Great Leap Forward was circulated to the Party elite. He lost his positions of power in 1959 and was never readmitted to the highest echelons of the CCP leadership.

Peng Zhen (1902–97)   Former mayor of Beijing and member of the CCP Central Committee and Politburo. Purged in the Cultural Revolution, Peng returned to a position of influence under Deng Xiaoping in the 1980s.

Qin Shi Huang Di   Founder of the Qin dynasty, he was the first ruler to use the title of emperor and is, therefore, often referred to as the First Emperor of China. His vast tomb, unearthed near Xian in the 1970s, attests to the military foundations of his empire as it contains thousands of clay (*terracotta*) warriors, a major resource for the study of the Qin period.

Sun Zhongshan (1866–1925)   Also known as Sun Yat-sen. Considered the Father of the Republic by both the Nationalist and Communist Parties, Sun served as President briefly in early 1912. The Nationalist Party grew from his earlier political organizations. He died before he was able to lead the Northern Expedition which he hoped would unify China.

Wang Guangmei (1922–)   American-born wife of Liu Shaoqi, Wang was detained in solitary confinement between 1967 and 1979, accused, like her husband, of opposing the Maoist revolution.

Wei Jingsheng (1950–)   Accused of opposing the Chinese government, Wei was sentenced to 15 years in prison in 1979. He served most of his sentence in solitary confinement. After his release, he once more spoke out against government polices and was re-arrested. In 1998 he was released on medical grounds and currently lives in the United States.

Yuan Shikai (1859–1916)   A Qing dynasty general who brokered the abdication of the child-emperor, Puyi, in 1911–12, paving the way for the new republic. Yuan used his position as head of the military to gain first the premiership of the new republic and then the presidency. His repressive government was unpopular. He died in 1916, the same year in which he planned to make himself emperor of China.

Zhao Ziyang (1919–)   Former Premier of China. Zhao began his political career holding offices in Guangzhou. He was hand-picked by Deng Xiaoping to serve as Premier in 1980 and to reform the commune system. Zhao's introduction of the contract responsibility system brought rapid agricultural expansion, and helped to launch China's economic revival after years of Maoist rule. Zhao was abruptly removed from office in 1989 after voicing support for China's students, and has remained under house arrest.

Zhou Enlai (1898–1976)   One of the most important and respected leaders of the twentieth century, Zhou joined the communist movement while a student in Europe and returned to support the CCP in the 1920s. Zhou held a number of high positions prior to 1949, and after the success of the revolution he served as China's Premier and as chief architect of China's foreign policy. Despite his ambiguous role in the Cultural Revolution, he is remembered as a force for moderation and reason during the Maoist period.

Zhu De (1886–1976)   General of the PLA. Zhu was Mao's close colleague and supporter from 1928 onwards and was largely responsible for handling military organization. General Zhu remained a loyal follower throughout his lifetime, preceding Mao in death by just a few months.

Zhu Rongji (1929–)   Prime Minister of China. Originally from Mao's home province of Hunan, Zhu joined the CCP in 1949 and graduated from Qinghua University in 1951. He held a number of positions in the State Planning Commission and other national-level governmental posts before becoming Shanghai's mayor in 1988, replacing Jiang Zemin with whom he had worked closely. In 1990, he was moved to Beijing and held a number of positions before being named Prime Minister in 1998 by President Jiang Zemin. His major task is to deepen China's economic reforms while maintaining political stability.

A GUIDE TO FURTHER READING

Primary Sources

There are a number of collections now available that provide translations of important documents on the People's Republic of China as well as a wealth of modern literature that vividly depicts life in contemporary China. Among the collections of primary documents currently available, the following are highly recommended: Cheng, Pei-kai and Michael Lestz, with Jonathan Spence (1999) *The Search for Modern China: A Documentary Collection* (New York: W.W. Norton), and, on the reform era, Orville Schell and David Shambaugh, eds (1999) *The China Reader: The Reform Era* (New York: Random House). For a day-by-day view of events in China, see the reports from FBIS [Foreign Broadcast Information Service] which are available from the US State Department in both hard copy and electronic form.

To understand the views of ordinary Chinese on such events as the Cultural Revolution and the changes which followed, see the interviews provided in Zhang Xinxin and Sang Ye (1987) *Chinese Lives: An Oral History of Contemporary China* (New York: Pantheon Press). Also of great interest are the frank interviews with men and women – on the Cultural Revolution and also everyday life in the 1990s – transcribed in Yarong Jiang and David Ashley (2000) *Mao's Children in the New China* (New York: Routledge).

For a lively set of essays by one of China's leading dissidents, see Fang Lizhi (1991) *Bringing Down the Great Wall: Writings on Science, Culture, and Democracy in China*, translated by James H. Williams (New York: Knopf). The outspoken Fang articulated the views of thousands of Chinese college students in the years leading up to 1989.

On the Tiananmen Square massacre, see the documents compiled in Michael Oksenberg, Lawrence R. Sullivan and Marc Lambert, eds (1990) *Beijing Spring 1989: Confrontation and Conflict: The Basic Documents* (Armonk, NY: M.E. Sharpe). For an assessment of the events by a Chinese dissident journalist, see Liu Binyan (1989) *Tell the World: What Happened in China and Why*, translated by Henry Epstein (New York: Pantheon Books). Additional government documents on the events of 'Beijing Spring' that are widely accepted as authentic outside China are available in Andrew J. Nathan and Perry Link, eds, and Liang Zhang, compiler (2001) *The Tiananmen Papers: Chinese Leadership's Decision to Use Force Against Their Own People – In Their Own Words* (New York: Public Affairs).

Secondary Sources

In addition to the primary sources listed above, many secondary sources today document the recent history of the PRC. For an account of change at the village level, see the interview-based account of Anita Chan, Richard Madsen and Jonathan Unger (1992) *Chen Village under Mao and Deng* (Los Angeles, CA: University of California Press). An anthropological account is provided in Sulamith Heins Potter and Jack M. Potter (1990) *China's Peasants: The Anthropology of a Revolution* (New York and Cambridge: Cambridge University Press).

For discussion of the government and politics, see Franz Schurmann (1966) *Ideology and Organization in Communist China* (Berkeley, CA: University of California Press) on the early years and, for more recent political organization, see the authoritative work of Kenneth Lieberthal (1995) *Governing China: From Revolution through Reform* (New York: W.W. Norton & Co).

There are numerous studies of the Cultural Revolution. Two that are particularly interesting include Lynn White III (1989) *Policies of Chaos: The Organizational Causes of Violence in China's Cultural Revolution* (Princeton, NJ: Princeton University Press) and Anne Thurston (1988) *Enemies of the People: The Ordeal of the Intellectuals in China's Great Cultural Revolution* (Cambridge: Harvard University Press). On the role of Mao's wife, see Roxanne Witke (1977) *Comrade Chiang Ch'ing* (Boston: Little Brown).

'Scar literature' detailing Chinese lives during this difficult time include Liang Heng and Judith Shapiro (1983) *Son of the Revolution* (New York: Vintage Books); Yue Daiyun, with Carolyn Wakeman (1985) *To the Storm: The Odyssey of a Revolutionary Chinese Woman* (Berkeley, CA: University of California Press); and Rae Yang (1997) *Spider Eaters* (Berkeley, CA: University of California Press). The earthy and blunt account of Ma Bo (1996) *Blood Red Sunset*, offers a biographical account of the deep disillusion of young men sent to gain revolutionary experience in the harsh setting of Inner Mongolia.

On population issues, useful volumes include Judith Banister (1987) *China's Changing Population* (Stanford, CA: Stanford University Press), and Penny Kane (1987) *The Second Billion: Population and Family Planning in China* (New York: Penguin Books).

In the past two decades, a wealth of material has appeared on women's status. These include biographical works, such as Chang Jung (1991) *Wild Swans: Three Daughters of China* (New York: Doubleday/Anchor Books), which provides an account of women's lives from the early twentieth century through the Cultural Revolution. For a Canadian-Chinese woman's account of China in the 1970s and 1980s, see the personal story of journalist Jan Wong (1997) *Red China Blues* (Toronto: Doubleday/Anchor Books).

Western scholars have examined many aspects of women's lives; trail-blazing studies include Gail Hershatter and Emily Honig (1988) *Personal Voices: Chinese Women in the 1980s* (Stanford, CA: Stanford University Press). Surveying changes for women since 1949 is Harriet Evans (1997) *Women and Sexuality in China* (New York: Continuum Press). Rural women are the focus of Tamara Jacka (1997) *Women's Work in Rural China* (Cambridge: Cambridge University Press). Broader discussion of changes in women's lives is the focus of Barbara Entwisle and Gail E. Henderson, eds (2000) *Re-drawing Boundaries: Work, Households, and Gender in China* (Berkeley, CA: University of California Press).

On the subject of women and men's private lives, see Liu Dalin, Man Lun Ng, Li Ping Zhou and Edwin J. Haeberle (1997) *Sexual Behavior in Modern China* (New York: Continuum Press), and for details on changes within the Chinese family, see Deborah Davis and Stevan Harrell, eds (1993) *Chinese Families in the Post-Mao Era* (Berkeley, CA: University of California Press). China's new consumerism is surveyed in Deborah S. Davis, ed. (2000) *The Consumer Revolution in Urban China* (Berkeley, CA: University of California Press), and in Conghua Li (1998) *China: The Consumer Revolution* (New York: Wiley). Related to consumerism and the changes that patterns of consumption suggest is the shift in popular culture that marks the 1990s: a provocative account of the latter is in Jianying Zha (1995) *China Pop: How Soap Operas, Tabloids, and Bestsellers are Transforming a Culture* (W.W. Norton).

A number of studies now focus on minority populations in China. Among these are Linda Benson and Ingvar Svanberg (1998) *China's Last Nomads: The History and Culture of China's Kazaks* (Armonk, NY: M.E. Sharpe), and Dru C. Gladney (1991) *Muslim Chinese* (Cambridge, MA: Harvard University Press). On Tibet, see Melvyn C. Goldstein (1997) *The Snow Lion and the Dragon* (Berkeley, CA: University of California Press), and Thomas Grunfeld, (1987) *The Making of Modern Tibet* (Armonk, NY: M.E. Sharpe). For a survey of minorities and issues related to their role in Chinese society, see Colin Mackerras (1995) *China's Minority Cultures: Identities and Integration since 1912* (New York and London: Longman).

Several books provide history and discussion of the status of religion in China. An excellent recent account of the state of Catholicism in reform-era China is Richard Madsen (1998) *China's Catholics: Tragedy and Hope in an Emerging Civil Society* (Berkeley, CA: University of California Press). On Protestant belief and comparison with other religious traditions in China, see Alan Hunter and Kimkwong Chan (1993) *Protestantism in Contemporary China* (Cambridge: Cambridge University Press). The Falungong, a religious movement banned in China in 1999, is the subject of books by practioners and the founder, Master Li Hongzhi. His works may be downloaded from the Internet free of charge.

The many changes which mark the two decades of the reform era are now treated in a number of informative, insightful accounts. Among the most valuable are Merle Goldman and Roderick MacFarquhar, eds (1999) *The Paradox of China's Post-Mao Reforms* (Cambridge, MA: Harvard University Press); Harry Harding (1987) *China's Second Revolution: Reform after Mao* (Washington, DC: Brookings Institute); Orville Schell (1988) *Discoes and Democracy: China in the Throes of Reform* (New York: Pantheon); Barrett McCormick and Jonathan Unger, eds (1996) *China after Socialism* (Armonk, NY: M.E. Sharpe); Andrew J. Nathan (1990) *China's Crisis: Dilemmas of Reform and Prospects for Democracy* (New York: Columbia University Press); and Elizabeth Perry and Mark Seldon, eds (2000) *Chinese Society: Change, Conflict and Resistance* (New York: Routledge).

Changes in specific areas have also been examined in the secondary literature. On the military, David Shambaugh and Richard H. Yang provide an edited volume (1997) *China's Military in Transition* (Oxford: Oxford University Press). An examination of the legal system is offered in Stanley B. Lubman (1999) *Bird in a Cage: Legal Reform after Mao* (Stanford, CA: Stanford University Press), and Jerome Cohen's now classic study, (1968) *The Criminal Process in the People's Republic of China 1949–1963: An Introduction* (Cambridge: Cambridge University Press).

China's many pressing environmental issues are of international concern. For a discussion of many of the major issues, see Michael B. McElroy, Christopher P. Nielsen and Peter Lyndon, eds (1998) *Energizing China: Reconciling Environmental*

Protection and Economic Growth (Cambridge, MA: Harvard University Press). Regarding the new dam on the Yangzi River in western China, see the critical book by Chinese writer Dai Qing (1994) *Yangtze! Yangtze!* (Toronto: Probe International).

Biographies of leading figures in the PRC include a range of books, from the more popular to the scholarly. On Mao, see Jonathan Spence (1999) *Mao Zedong* (New York and London: Penguin); Ross Terrill (1980; re-issued 1993) *Mao: A Biography* (New York: Simon and Schuster); and Philip Short (1999) *Mao: A Life* (New York: Henry Holt and Co.). An extremely critical and highly personal memoir of Mao can be found in Dr Li Zhisui (1994) *The Private Life of Chairman Mao* (New York: Random House). On the life of reformer Deng Xiaoping, see Richard Evans (1995) *Deng Xiaoping and the Making of Modern China* (London: Penguin Books), and Benjamin Yang (1998) *Deng: A Political Biography* (Armonk, NY: M.E. Sharpe). The only English-language biography of President Jiang Zemin is the highly readable account by Bruce Gilley (1998) *Tiger on the Brink: Jiang Zemin and China's New Elite* (Berkeley, CA: University of California Press).

Literature on Hong Kong and Taiwan offers the opportunity to assess changes in China in comparison to Chinese areas with very different economic histories. On Taiwan, interesting studies of the past and contemporary issues include A-Chin Hsiao (2000) *Contemporary Taiwanese Cultural Nationalism* (London: Routledge); Murray Rubenstein, ed. (1994) *The Other Taiwan: 1945 to the Present* (Armonk, NY: M.E. Sharpe); and Robert M. Marsh (1996) *The Great Transformation: Social Change in Taipei, Taiwan, since the 1960s* (Armonk, NY: M.E. Sharpe). Hong Kong's return to the PRC was the focus of various studies, among them the essays in Ming K. Chan, ed. (1994) *Precarious Balance: Hong Kong between China and Britain, 1982–1992* (Armonk, NY: M.E. Sharpe). For a discussion of the impact of Chinese sovereignty, see the articles in Gungwu Wang and John Wong, eds (1999) *Hong Kong in China: The Challenges of Transition* (Singapore: Times Academic Press).

REFERENCES

Becker, Jasper (1996) *Hungry Ghosts: China's Secret Famine*. London: John Murray.

Fang Lizhi (1991) *Bringing Down the Great Wall: Writings on Science, Culture and Democracy in China*. Translated by James H. Williams. New York: W.W. Norton.

Gao Yuan (1987) *Born Red: A Chronicle of the Cultural Revolution*. Stanford, CA: Stanford University Press.

Gilley, Bruce (1999) 'Jiang Zemin: On the Right Side of History?', *Current History*, September, 249–53.

Gladney, Dru C. (1998) *Ethnic Identity in China*. New York: Harcourt Brace & Company, 12–13.

Goldman, Merle and Roderick MacFarquhar, eds (1999) *The Paradox of China's Post-Mao Reforms*. Cambridge, MA: Harvard University Press.

Goldstein, Melvyn C. (1997) *The Snow Lion and the Dragon: China, Tibet, and the Dalai Lama*. Berkeley, CA: University of California Press.

Greenhalgh, Susan (1994) 'Conrolling Births and Bodies in Village China', *American Ethnologist*, 21 (February), 3–30.

Jacka, Tamara (1997) *Women's Work in Rural China*. Cambridge: Cambridge University Press.

Jiang Yurong and David Ashley (2000) *Mao's Children in the New China: Voices from the Red Guard Generation*. New York: Routledge.

Lee, Ching Kwan (1998) *Gender and the South China Miracle: Two Worlds of Factory Women*. Berkeley, CA: University of California Press.

Liang Heng and Judith Shapiro (1983) *Son of the Revolution*. New York: Vintage Books.

Ma Bo (1996) *Blood Red Sunset: A Memoir of the Chinese Cultural Revolution*. Translated by Howard Goldblatt. New York: Penguin Books.

MacFarquhar, Roderick, ed. (1997) *The Politics of China: The Eras of Mao and Deng*. New York: Cambridge University Press,

Mackerras, Colin (1998) *China in Transformation 1900–1949*. New York and London: Longman.

Meisener, Maurice (1999), 'China's Communist Revolution: A Half-Century Perspective', *Current History*, 98:629 (September), 243–8.

Parris, Kristen (1999) 'The Rise of Private Business Interests', in Merle Goldman and Roderick MacFarquhar, eds, *The Paradox of China's Post-Mao Reforms*. Cambridge, MA: Harvard University Press, 262–82.

Selden, Mark (ed.) (1979) *The People's Republic of China: A Documentary History of Revolutionary Change*. New York: Monthly Press Review, 187–93.

Seymour, James and Richard Anderson (1998) *New Ghosts, Old Ghosts: Prisons and Labor Reform Camps in China*. Armonk, NY: M.E. Sharpe.

Seymour, James (1999) 'Human Rights, Repression, and "Stability"', *Current History*, 98:629 (September), 281–5.

Short, Philip (1999) *Mao: A Life*. New York: Henry Holt and Co.

Spence, Jonathan (1990) *The Search for Modern China*. New York: W.W. Norton & Co.

Spence, Jonathan (1999) *Mao Zedong*. New York: Penguin.

Terrill, Ross (1993) *Mao: A Biography*. New York: Simon and Schuster (first published in 1980).

Uhalley, Jr., Stephen (1988) *A History of the Chinese Communist Party*. Stanford, CA: Stanford University Press.

Yue Daiyun, with Carolyn Wakeman (1985) *To the Storm: The Odyssey of a Chinese Woman Revolutionary*. Berkeley, CA: University of California Press.

INDEX

SEMINAR STUDIES IN HISTORY

General Editors: Clive Emsley & Gordon Martel

The series was founded by Patrick Richardson in 1966. Between 1980 and 1996 Roger Lockyer edited the series before handing over to Clive Emsley (Professor of History at the Open University) and Gordon Martel (Professor of International History at the University of Northern British Columbia, Canada and Senior Research Fellow at De Montfort University).

MEDIEVAL ENGLAND

The Pre-Reformation Church in England 1400–1530 (Second edition)
Christopher Harper-Bill   0 582 28989 0

Lancastrians and Yorkists: The Wars of the Roses
David R Cook   0 582 35384 X

Family and Kinship in England 1450–1800
Will Coster   0 582 35717 9

TUDOR ENGLAND

Henry VII (Third edition)
Roger Lockyer & Andrew Thrush   0 582 20912 9

Henry VIII (Second edition)
M D Palmer   0 582 35437 4

Tudor Rebellions (Fourth edition)
Anthony Fletcher & Diarmaid MacCulloch   0 582 28990 4

The Reign of Mary I (Second edition)
Robert Tittler   0 582 06107 5

Early Tudor Parliaments 1485–1558
Michael A R Graves   0 582 03497 3

The English Reformation 1530–1570
W J Sheils   0 582 35398 X

Elizabethan Parliaments 1559–1601 (Second edition)
Michael A R Graves   0 582 29196 8

England and Europe 1485–1603 (Second edition)
Susan Doran   0 582 28991 2

The Church of England 1570–1640
Andrew Foster   0 582 35574 5

STUART BRITAIN

Social Change and Continuity: England 1550–1750 (Second edition)
Barry Coward 0 582 29442 8

James I (Second edition)
S J Houston 0 582 20911 0

The English Civil War 1640–1649
Martyn Bennett 0 582 35392 0

Charles I, 1625–1640
Brian Quintrell 0 582 00354 7

The English Republic 1649–1660 (Second edition)
Toby Barnard 0 582 08003 7

Radical Puritans in England 1550–1660
R J Acheson 0 582 35515 X

The Restoration and the England of Charles II (Second edition)
John Miller 0 582 29223 9

The Glorious Revolution (Second edition)
John Miller 0 582 29222 0

EARLY MODERN EUROPE

The Renaissance (Second edition)
Alison Brown 0 582 30781 3

The Emperor Charles V
Martyn Rady 0 582 35475 7

French Renaissance Monarchy: Francis I and Henry II (Second edition)
Robert Knecht 0 582 28707 3

The Protestant Reformation in Europe
Andrew Johnston 0 582 07020 1

The French Wars of Religion 1559–1598 (Second edition)
Robert Knecht 0 582 28533 X

Phillip II
Geoffrey Woodward 0 582 07232 8

The Thirty Years' War
Peter Limm 0 582 35373 4

Louis XIV
Peter Campbell 0 582 01770 X

Spain in the Seventeenth Century
Graham Darby 0 582 07234 4

Peter the Great
William Marshall 0 582 00355 5

EUROPE 1789–1918

Britain and the French Revolution
Clive Emsley   0 582 36961 4

Revolution and Terror in France 1789–1795 (Second edition)
D G Wright   0 582 00379 2

Napoleon and Europe
D G Wright   0 582 35457 9

The Abolition of Serfdom in Russia, 1762–1907
David Moon   0 582 29486 X

Nineteenth-Century Russia: Opposition to Autocracy
Derek Offord   0 582 35767 5

The Constitutional Monarchy in France 1814–48
Pamela Pilbeam   0 582 31210 8

The 1848 Revolutions (Second edition)
Peter Jones   0 582 06106 7

The Italian Risorgimento
M Clark   0 582 00353 9

Bismarck & Germany 1862–1890 (Second edition)
D G Williamson   0 582 29321 9

Imperial Germany 1890–1918
Ian Porter, Ian Armour and Roger Lockyer   0 582 03496 5

The Dissolution of the Austro-Hungarian Empire 1867–1918 (Second edition)
John W Mason   0 582 29466 5

Second Empire and Commune: France 1848–1871 (Second edition)
William H C Smith   0 582 28705 7

France 1870–1914 (Second edition)
Robert Gildea   0 582 29221 2

The Scramble for Africa (Second edition)
M E Chamberlain   0 582 36881 2

Late Imperial Russia 1890–1917
John F Hutchinson   0 582 32721 0

The First World War
Stuart Robson   0 582 31556 5

Austria, Prussia and Germany, 1806–1871
John Breuilly   0 582 43739 3

EUROPE SINCE 1918

The Russian Revolution (Second edition)
Anthony Wood   0 582 35559 1

Lenin's Revolution: Russia, 1917–1921
David Marples   0 582 31917 X

Stalin and Stalinism (Second edition)
Martin McCauley 0 582 27658 6

The Weimar Republic (Second edition)
John Hiden 0 582 28706 5

The Inter-War Crisis 1919–1939
Richard Overy 0 582 35379 3

Fascism and the Right in Europe, 1919–1945
Martin Blinkhorn 0 582 07021 X

Spain's Civil War (Second edition)
Harry Browne 0 582 28988 2

The Third Reich (Third edition)
D G Williamson 0 582 20914 5

The Origins of the Second World War (Second edition)
R J Overy 0 582 29085 6

The Second World War in Europe
Paul MacKenzie 0 582 32692 3

The French at War, 1934–1944
Nicholas Atkin 0 582 36899 5

Anti-Semitism before the Holocaust
Albert S Lindemann 0 582 36964 9

The Holocaust: The Third Reich and the Jews
David Engel 0 582 32720 2

Germany from Defeat to Partition, 1945–1963
D G Williamson 0 582 29218 2

Britain and Europe since 1945
Alex May 0 582 30778 3

Eastern Europe 1945–1969: From Stalinism to Stagnation
Ben Fowkes 0 582 32693 1

Eastern Europe since 1970
Bülent Gökay 0 582 32858 6

The Khrushchev Era, 1953–1964
Martin McCauley 0 582 27776 0

NINETEENTH-CENTURY BRITAIN

Britain before the Reform Acts: Politics and Society 1815–1832
Eric J Evans 0 582 00265 6

Parliamentary Reform in Britain c. 1770–1918
Eric J Evans 0 582 29467 3

Democracy and Reform 1815–1885
D G Wright 0 582 31400 3

Poverty and Poor Law Reform in Nineteenth-Century Britain, 1834–1914:
From Chadwick to Booth
David Englander　　　　　　　　　　　　　　　　　　　　　0 582 31554 9

The Birth of Industrial Britain: Economic Change, 1750–1850
Kenneth Morgan　　　　　　　　　　　　　　　　　　　　　0 582 29833 4

Chartism (Third edition)
Edward Royle　　　　　　　　　　　　　　　　　　　　　　0 582 29080 5

Peel and the Conservative Party 1830–1850
Paul Adelman　　　　　　　　　　　　　　　　　　　　　　0 582 35557 5

Gladstone, Disraeli and later Victorian Politics (Third edition)
Paul Adelman　　　　　　　　　　　　　　　　　　　　　　0 582 29322 7

Britain and Ireland: From Home Rule to Independence
Jeremy Smith　　　　　　　　　　　　　　　　　　　　　　0 582 30193 9

TWENTIETH-CENTURY BRITAIN

The Rise of the Labour Party 1880–1945 (Third edition)
Paul Adelman　　　　　　　　　　　　　　　　　　　　　　0 582 29210 7

The Conservative Party and British Politics 1902–1951
Stuart Ball　　　　　　　　　　　　　　　　　　　　　　　0 582 08002 9

The Decline of the Liberal Party 1910–1931 (Second edition)
Paul Adelman　　　　　　　　　　　　　　　　　　　　　　0 582 27733 7

The British Women's Suffrage Campaign 1866–1928
Harold L Smith　　　　　　　　　　　　　　　　　　　　　0 582 29811 3

War & Society in Britain 1899–1948
Rex Pope　　　　　　　　　　　　　　　　　　　　　　　　0 582 03531 7

The British Economy since 1914: A Study in Decline?
Rex Pope　　　　　　　　　　　　　　　　　　　　　　　　0 582 30194 7

Unemployment in Britain between the Wars
Stephen Constantine　　　　　　　　　　　　　　　　　　　0 582 35232 0

The Attlee Governments 1945–1951
Kevin Jefferys　　　　　　　　　　　　　　　　　　　　　　0 582 06105 9

The Conservative Governments 1951–1964
Andrew Boxer　　　　　　　　　　　　　　　　　　　　　　0 582 20913 7

Britain under Thatcher
Anthony Seldon and Daniel Collings　　　　　　　　　　　　　0 582 31714 2

Britain and Empire, 1880–1945
Dane Kennedy　　　　　　　　　　　　　　　　　　　　　　0 582 41493 8

INTERNATIONAL HISTORY

The Eastern Question 1774–1923 (Second edition)
A L Macfie   0 582 29195 X

India 1885–1947: The Unmaking of an Empire
Ian Copland   0 582 38173 8

The Origins of the First World War (Second edition)
Gordon Martel   0 582 28697 2

The United States and the First World War
Jennifer D Keene   0 582 35620 2

Anti-Semitism before the Holocaust
Albert S Lindemann   0 582 36964 9

The Origins of the Cold War, 1941–1949 (Second edition)
Martin McCauley   0 582 27659 4

Russia, America and the Cold War, 1949–1991
Martin McCauley   0 582 27936 4

The Arab–Israeli Conflict
Kirsten E Schulze   0 582 31646 4

The United Nations since 1945: Peacekeeping and the Cold War
Norrie MacQueen   0 582 35673 3

Decolonisation: The British Experience since 1945
Nicholas J White   0 582 29087 2

The Origins of the Vietnam War
Fredrik Logevall   0 582 31918 8

The Vietnam War
Mitchell Hall   0 582 32859 4

WORLD HISTORY

China in Transformation 1900–1949
Colin Mackerras   0 582 31209 4

Japan Faces the World, 1925–1952
Mary L Hanneman   0 582 36898 7

Japan in Transformation, 1952–2000
Jeff Kingston   0 582 41875 5

China since 1949
Linda Benson   0 582 35722 5

US HISTORY

American Abolitionists
Stanley Harrold   0 582 35738 1

The American Civil War, 1861–1865
Reid Mitchell   0 582 31973 0

America in the Progressive Era, 1890–1914
Lewis L Gould   0 582 35671 7

The United States and the First World War
Jennifer D Keene   0 582 35620 2

The Truman Years, 1945–1953
Mark S Byrnes   0 582 32904 3

The Korean War
Steven Hugh Lee   0 582 31988 9

The Origins of the Vietnam War
Fredrik Logevall   0 582 31918 8

The Vietnam War
Mitchell Hall   0 582 32859 4